This book belongs to:

_____

LEISURE ARTS, INC.
Little Rock, Arkansas

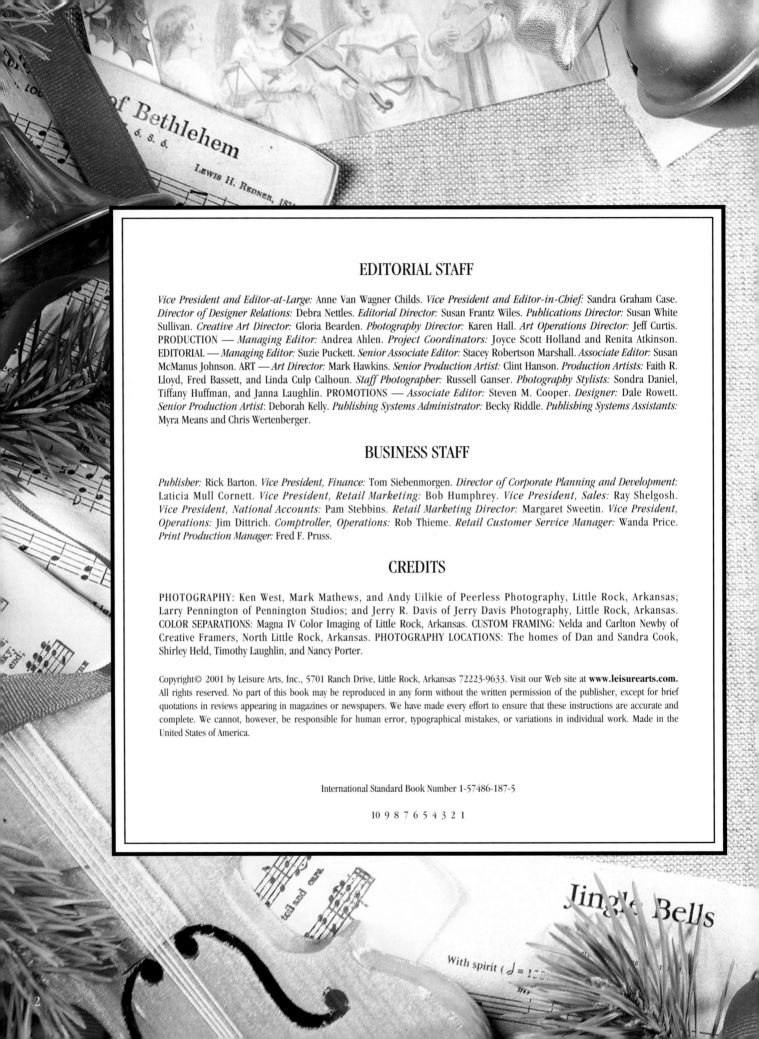

EDITORIAL STAFF

Vice President and Editor-at-Large: Anne Van Wagner Childs. *Vice President and Editor-in-Chief:* Sandra Graham Case. *Director of Designer Relations:* Debra Nettles. *Editorial Director:* Susan Frantz Wiles. *Publications Director:* Susan White Sullivan. *Creative Art Director:* Gloria Bearden. *Photography Director:* Karen Hall. *Art Operations Director:* Jeff Curtis. PRODUCTION — *Managing Editor:* Andrea Ahlen. *Project Coordinators:* Joyce Scott Holland and Renita Atkinson. EDITORIAL — *Managing Editor:* Suzie Puckett. *Senior Associate Editor:* Stacey Robertson Marshall. *Associate Editor:* Susan McManus Johnson. ART — *Art Director:* Mark Hawkins. *Senior Production Artist:* Clint Hanson. *Production Artists:* Faith R. Lloyd, Fred Bassett, and Linda Culp Calhoun. *Staff Photographer:* Russell Ganser. *Photography Stylists:* Sondra Daniel, Tiffany Huffman, and Janna Laughlin. PROMOTIONS — *Associate Editor:* Steven M. Cooper. *Designer:* Dale Rowett. *Senior Production Artist*: Deborah Kelly. *Publishing Systems Administrator:* Becky Riddle. *Publishing Systems Assistants:* Myra Means and Chris Wertenberger.

BUSINESS STAFF

Publisher: Rick Barton. *Vice President, Finance:* Tom Siebenmorgen. *Director of Corporate Planning and Development:* Laticia Mull Cornett. *Vice President, Retail Marketing:* Bob Humphrey. *Vice President, Sales:* Ray Shelgosh. *Vice President, National Accounts:* Pam Stebbins. *Retail Marketing Director:* Margaret Sweetin. *Vice President, Operations:* Jim Dittrich. *Comptroller, Operations:* Rob Thieme. *Retail Customer Service Manager:* Wanda Price. *Print Production Manager:* Fred F. Pruss.

CREDITS

PHOTOGRAPHY: Ken West, Mark Mathews, and Andy Uilkie of Peerless Photography, Little Rock, Arkansas; Larry Pennington of Pennington Studios; and Jerry R. Davis of Jerry Davis Photography, Little Rock, Arkansas. COLOR SEPARATIONS: Magna IV Color Imaging of Little Rock, Arkansas. CUSTOM FRAMING: Nelda and Carlton Newby of Creative Framers, North Little Rock, Arkansas. PHOTOGRAPHY LOCATIONS: The homes of Dan and Sandra Cook, Shirley Held, Timothy Laughlin, and Nancy Porter.

International Standard Book Number 1-57486-187-5

10 9 8 7 6 5 4 3 2 1

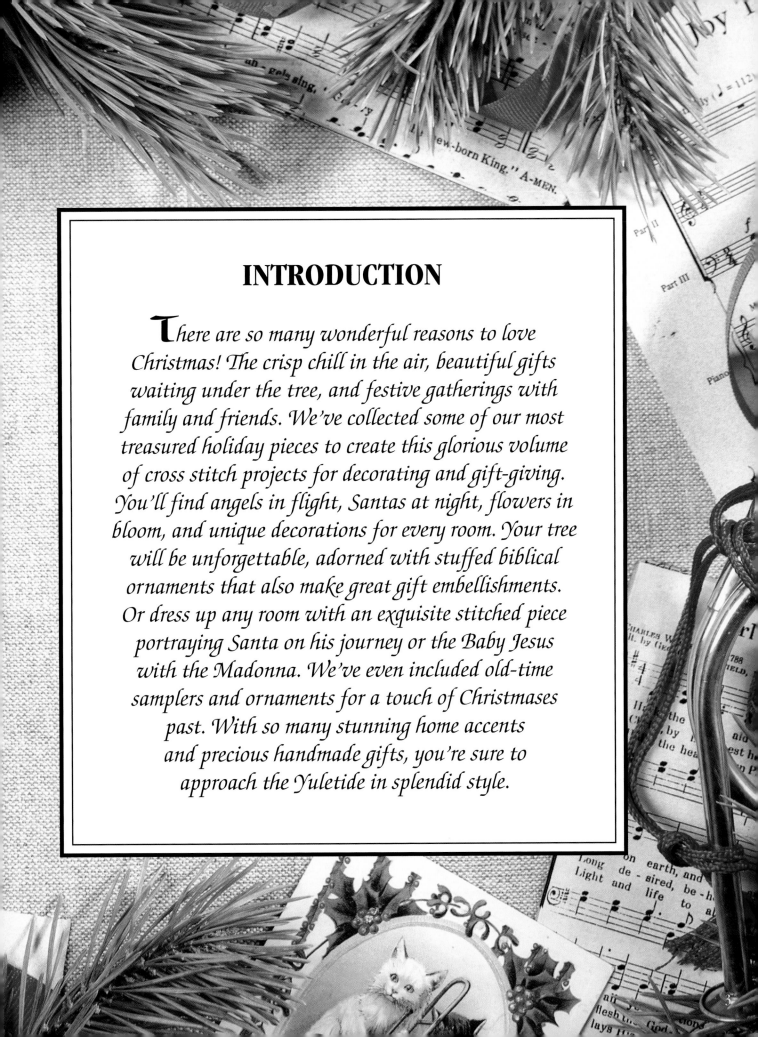

INTRODUCTION

There are so many wonderful reasons to love Christmas! The crisp chill in the air, beautiful gifts waiting under the tree, and festive gatherings with family and friends. We've collected some of our most treasured holiday pieces to create this glorious volume of cross stitch projects for decorating and gift-giving. You'll find angels in flight, Santas at night, flowers in bloom, and unique decorations for every room. Your tree will be unforgettable, adorned with stuffed biblical ornaments that also make great gift embellishments. Or dress up any room with an exquisite stitched piece portraying Santa on his journey or the Baby Jesus with the Madonna. We've even included old-time samplers and ornaments for a touch of Christmases past. With so many stunning home accents and precious handmade gifts, you're sure to approach the Yuletide in splendid style.

TABLE OF CONTENTS

REINDEER SLEIGH

On Dasher, on Dancer,
on Donder, on Blitzen —
Santa has much work to do
to finish his merry gift-giving!
Capture the magic of his Christmas
journey with this three-dimensional
reindeer sleigh. Accented with tiny
jingle bells and gold cord "reins,"
the stuffed display stands on its
own for a wonderful holiday
touch anywhere in your home.

Charts on pages 44-47

CHRISTMAS JOURNEY

Making his way through the dark and snowy night, Santa still has many treasures left to bestow on good little boys and girls. Guided by the glow of the lamplight, the crimson-cloaked gentleman will bring joy to young and old in this heartwarming stitched piece.

Chart on pages 48-49

NOEL NATURALS

Capture all the flora of Christmas —
including mistletoe, poinsettias, and holly
— with this timeless collection taken
straight from nature. Sprinkle your
tree with these elegant cording-trimmed
ornaments, or give them away as
exquisite gifts or package decorations.

Charts on pages 50-51

O COME, ALL YE FAITHFUL

Yuletide hymns are perfect reminders of the true meaning of the season. Accented with holly, berries, and shimmering gold beads, a classic holiday song is presented in resplendent detail on this delicate stitched piece. May it serve your family as a beautiful remembrance of what Christmas is all about.

Chart on pages 52-53

$\mathcal{T}$he joyous strains of Yuletide carols will be brought to mind when family and guests admire these rich ornaments and embellished pillows. Adorned with musical notes, ribbon, and greenery, these pieces make excellent holiday accents and gifts.

Charts on pages 54-55

Charts on page 55

WOODLAND SANTA

Surrounded by his charming
woodland friends, Saint Nick totes his pack
full of fabulous gifts for sharing with one and
all. Personalize the cuff of the handsome
stocking, and let this merry gentleman carry
a bounty of treats to your special one.

Chart on pages 56-62

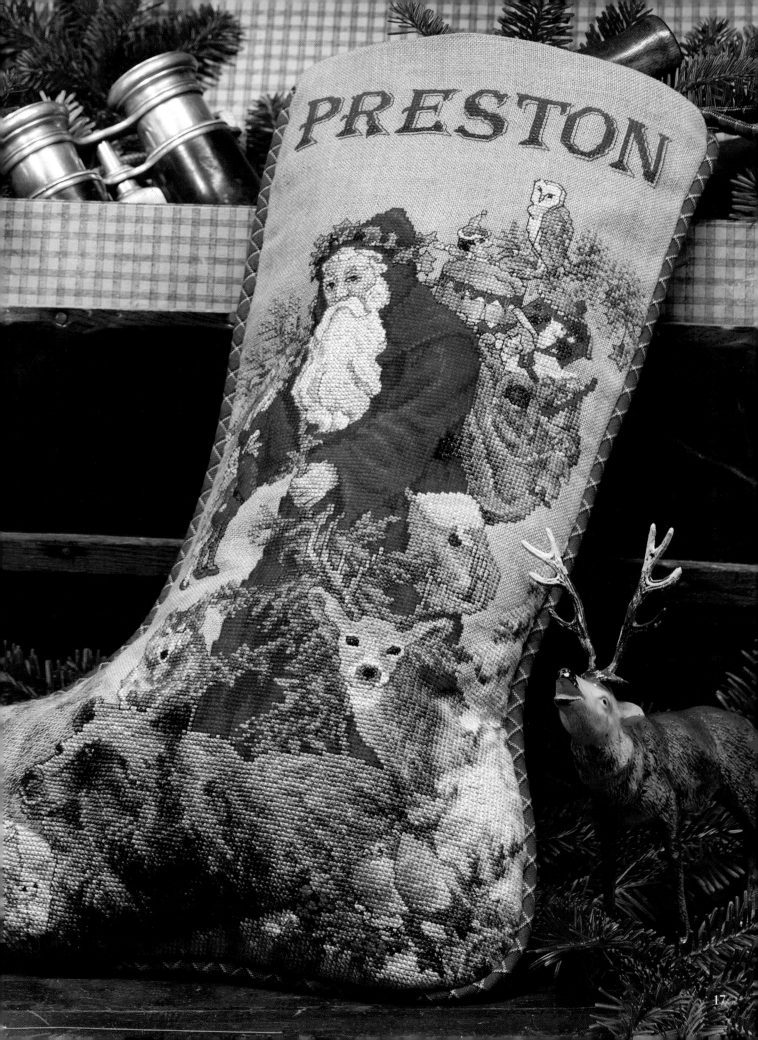

MERRIE ALPHABET

here are twenty-six wonderful reasons to adore Christmas! Each letter of the alphabet is illustrated by a tiny treasure — from an angelic messenger to a zebra in festive attire. Bordered with mini motifs and candy-cane stripes, our spirited sampler brings the childlike innocence of the Yuletide to your home. What a lovely way to wish a "Merrie Christmas to All!"

Chart on pages 64-69

*With or without their accompanying letters,
joyous designs from the alphabet sampler
also make special little gifts to treasure.*

Chart on pages 64-69

home sweet home

Bring a bit of an old-fashioned Christmas to your holiday home with our elaborate pillow band. Leaf and berry designs swirl about a timeless saying that is appropriate for any time of year. Simply slip the band around a throw pillow to create an instant decoration for your favorite sofa or chair.

Chart on pages 70-71

GLORY
OF THE
LORD

Remember the true meaning
of the season with our glorious
sampler worthy of passing down
from generation to generation.
The Bible quote is surrounded
by a frame of leaves and flowers
stitched in warm mauves and
greens. Not only can you enjoy
this beautiful piece throughout
the holidays — it's a perfect
year-round way to give
thanks to the Lord.

Chart on page 72

Spread the joy of our most holy holiday with adornments fashioned in honor of treasured stories from the Bible. Hang the ruffled angel pillow on a chair or doorknob for a quick accent, and sprinkle your tree or packages with stuffed ornaments dressed up with corded trim and tassels.

Charts on pages 73-74

Jonah & the whale

Charts on page 73

27

FESTIVE TREE

Glistening bead garlands and a charming little angel give beautiful depth to an elegant evergreen. With a flutter of tiny wings, more golden seraphim alight on a pretty pair of bookmarks. They join the smiling cherubim in their peaceful vigilance over the best of all books.

Charts on pages 75-77

CHORUS OF ANGELS

Share a Victorian Christmas with family and friends by displaying this glorious angel piece. Framed by an intricate border, magnificent seraphs bring the joyous news of the Messiah's birth. What a lovely way to wish someone an "angelic" holiday!

Chart on pages 78-83

Chart on pages 79-81

Chart on page 79

Though rarely allowing themselves to be seen, these heavenly hosts happily grace our holiday gifts. A trio of stellar beauties and two exuberant cherubs add Yuletide joy to luxurious pillows. The regal angel ornament brings blessings to Christmas celebrations. And inside a gilded frame, a devoted guardian tenderly watches over the sleep of her small charge.

Chart on pages 79, 81-82

BEARING GIFTS

His soulful eyes and rosy cheeks tell the age-old story of Saint Nick, a kind and gentle giver of gifts. In this tender stitched piece, Santa cradles a cuddly teddy bear, perhaps a gift for the next little boy on his list.

Chart on pages 86-87

Gifts of warmth, love, and joy; let them delight the hearts of all!
A gentle Father Christmas afghan or a personalized teddy bear
stocking will remind someone how very much you care.

Chart on pages 86-87

Charts on pages 88-89

MADONNA AND CHILD

It brings such joy to regale the remarkable story of our Saviour's birth at Christmastime. Invite a little of this special magic into your home with an exquisite portrayal of the Madonna swaddling her newborn Son. It's sure to become a treasured heirloom that your family will enjoy for years to come.

Chart on pages 90-91

CHRISTMAS BOTANICALS

holly and poinsettias are true reminders that the Yuletide is near. Naturally rich in the holiday colors of red and green, these beautiful botanical pieces can be enjoyed long after Christmas has passed.

Charts on pages 92-93

CHILDREN IN THE SNOW

Children love the snow, and as soon as it begins to fall, this delightful white frost seems to bring out the child in all of us. Capture the happiness of younger days with our whimsical piece featuring laughing youngsters enjoying a snowball fight. It's sure to bring back precious childhood memories to the truly young at heart.

Chart on pages 94-95

REINDEER SLEIGH

Reindeer Sleigh Standing Figures (shown on pages 6-7, Reindeer charts on pages 46-47): The Santa and sleigh were stitched on a 14" square of Dirty Aida (14 ct). Three strands of floss were used for Cross Stitch and 1 strand for Backstitch, unless otherwise noted in the color key. Use 1 strand of DMC 729 floss to attach 6mm jingle bells to sleigh and each reindeer.

FINISHING INSTRUCTIONS

For each stuffed figure, you will need Dirty Aida for backing, polyester fiberfill, tracing paper, pencil, fabric marking pencil, plastic sandwich bag, and aquarium gravel.

Cut a piece of Dirty Aida same size as stitched piece for backing. Matching right sides and raw edges and leaving bottom edge open, sew stitched piece and backing together 2 squares from edge of design as shown in **Fig. 1**. Leaving a 1/4" seam allowance, cut out figure. Clip seam allowances at curves; turn figure right side out, carefully pushing curves outward. Trim bottom edges of figure 1/2" from bottom of design. Press raw edges 1/4" to wrong side; stuff figure with polyester fiberfill up to 1 1/2" from opening.

For base pattern, set figure on tracing paper and draw around base of figure. Add a 1/2" seam allowance to pattern; cut out pattern. Place pattern on piece of Aida. Use fabric marking pencil to draw around pattern; cut out on drawn line. Baste around base piece 1/2" from raw edge; press raw edges to wrong side along basting line.

To weight bottom of figure, fill a plastic sandwich bag with a small amount of aquarium gravel. Place bag of gravel into opening of figure.

Pin wrong side of base piece over opening. Whipstitch in place, adding polyester fiberfill as necessary to fill bottom of figure. Remove basting threads.

Using 1/16" dia. gold cord for reins, refer to photo and tack cord in place.

Fig. 1

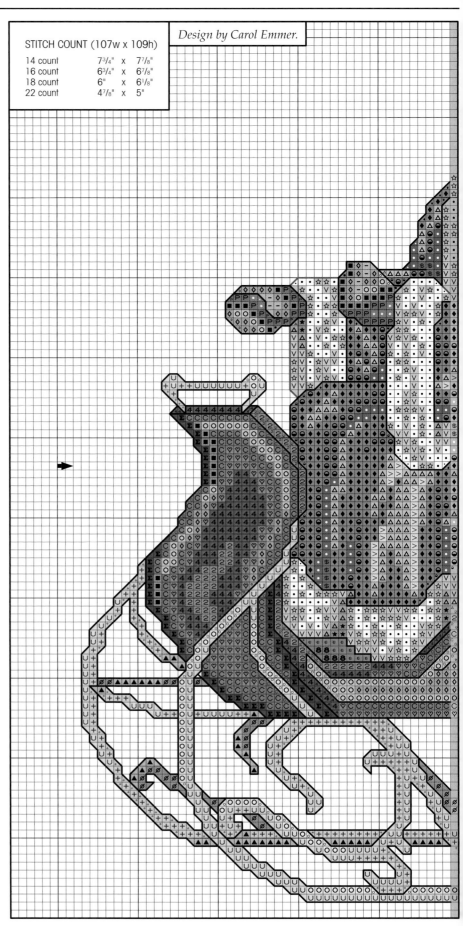

STITCH COUNT (107w x 109h)			
14 count	7 3/4"	x	7 7/8"
16 count	6 3/4"	x	6 7/8"
18 count	6"	x	6 1/8"
22 count	4 7/8"	x	5"

Design by Carol Emmer.

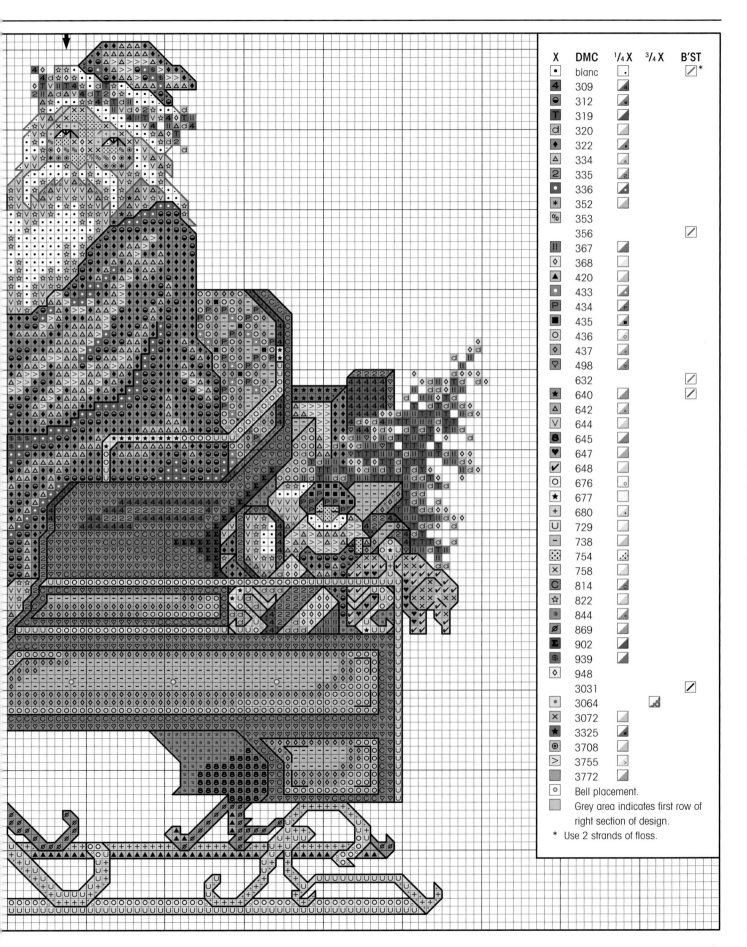

X	DMC	¼ X	¾ X	B'ST
•	blanc	•		╱ *
4	309	4		
◒	312	◒		
T	319	◪		
d	320	◪		
◆	322	◢		
△	334	△		
2	335	2		
◉	336	◢		
*	352	◪		
%	353			
	356			╱
‖	367	◪		
◇	368	◪		
▲	420	◪		
◙	433	◪		
P	434	◪		
■	435	■		
O	436	◦		
◇	437	◇		
♡	498	◪		
	632			╱
★	640	◪		╱
△	642	△		
V	644	◪		
8	645	◪		
♥	647	◪		
✔	648	◪		
O	676	◦		
★	677			
+	680	+		
U	729	◪		
-	738	◪		
⠒	754	⠒		
✕	758	◪		
C	814	◪		
☆	822	◪		
◉	844	◪		
∅	869	◪		
Σ	902	◪		
$	939	◪		
◇	948			
	3031			╱
⦿	3064		◪	
✕	3072	◪		
⊠	3325	◢		
◉	3708	◪		
>	3755	>		
▨	3772	◪		
◎	Bell placement.			
▨	Grey area indicates first row of right section of design.			
*	Use 2 strands of floss.			

REINDEER SLEIGh

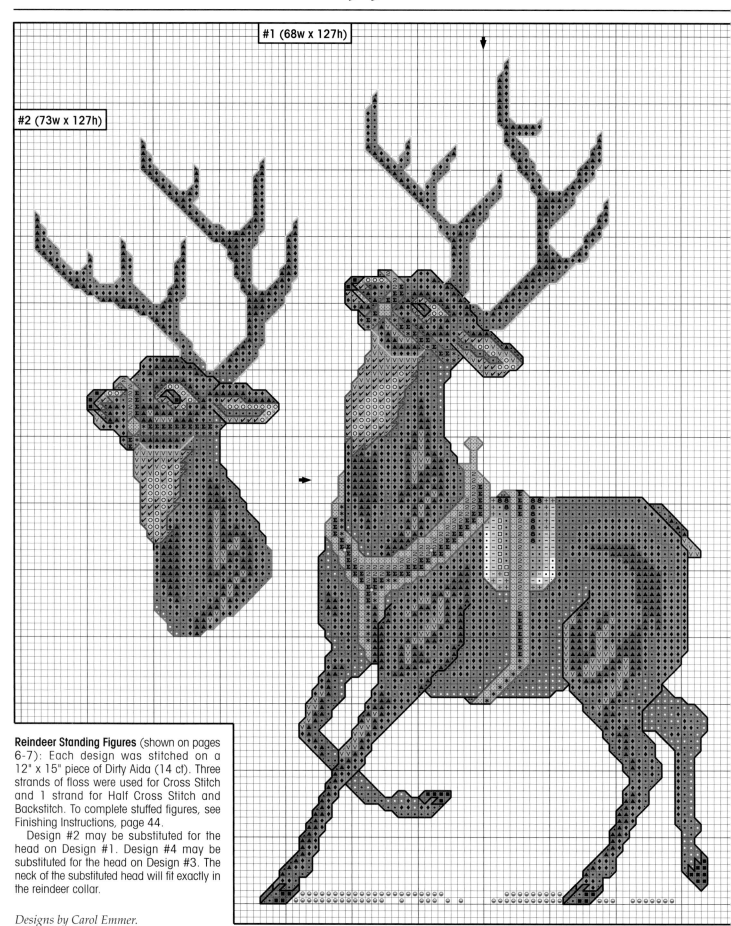

#1 (68w x 127h)

#2 (73w x 127h)

Reindeer Standing Figures (shown on pages 6-7): Each design was stitched on a 12" x 15" piece of Dirty Aida (14 ct). Three strands of floss were used for Cross Stitch and 1 strand for Half Cross Stitch and Backstitch. To complete stuffed figures, see Finishing Instructions, page 44.

Design #2 may be substituted for the head on Design #1. Design #4 may be substituted for the head on Design #3. The neck of the substituted head will fit exactly in the reindeer collar.

Designs by Carol Emmer.

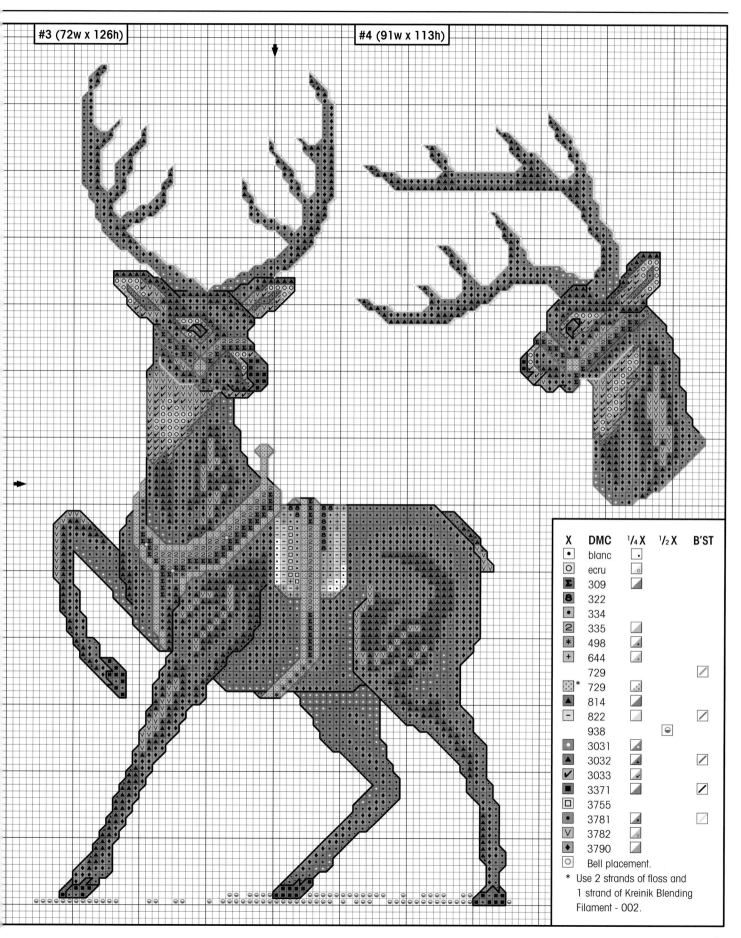

#3 (72w x 126h) #4 (91w x 113h)

X	DMC	¼ X	½ X	B'ST
•	blanc	•		
O	ecru	o		
Σ	309	◪		
8	322			
•	334			
2	335	◪		
*	498	◪		
+	644	◪		
	729			◪
⊡ *	729	◪		
▲	814	◪		◪
-	822	◪		◪
	938		◉	
⊡	3031			
▲	3032	◪		◪
✔	3033	◪		
■	3371	◪		◪
⊡	3755			
•	3781	◪		◪
V	3782	◪		
◆	3790	◪		
⊙	Bell placement.			

* Use 2 strands of floss and
  1 strand of Kreinik Blending
  Filament - 002.

CHRISTMAS JOURNEY

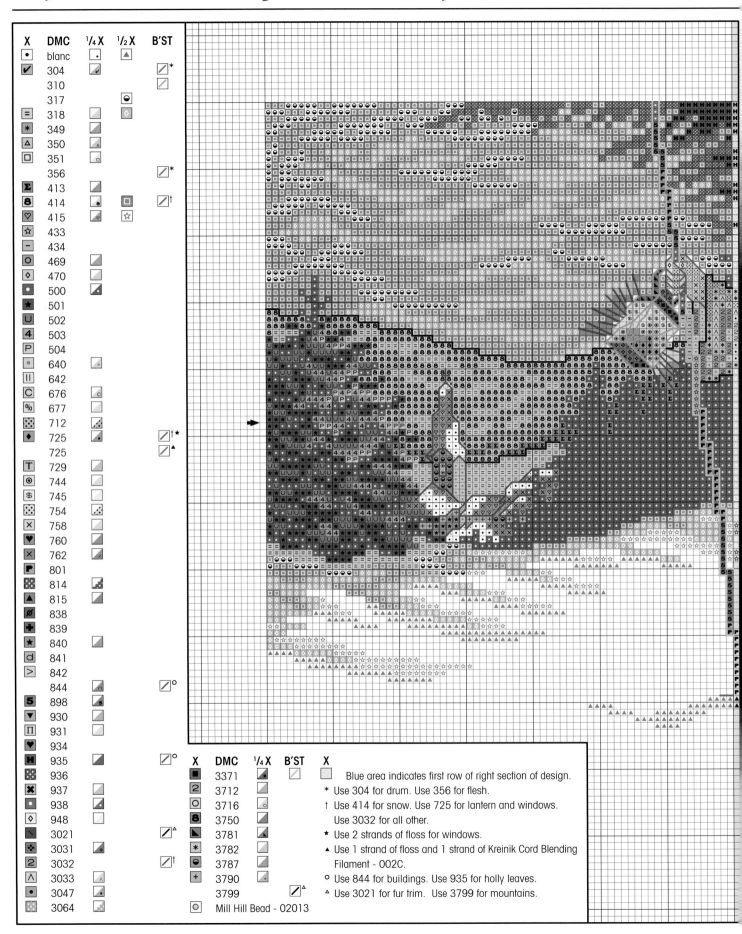

X	DMC	¼X	½X	B'ST
•	blanc	•	▲	
✔	304	✔		╱*
	310			╱
	317		◖	
=	318		◈	
✳	349			
△	350	△		
☐	351	☐		
	356			╱*
Σ	413			
8	414	8	☐	╱†
♡	415	♡	☆	
☆	433			
–	434			
O	469			
◇	470			
◉	500			
★	501			
U	502			
4	503			
P	504			
⊙	640			
‖	642			
C	676	C		
%	677			
▒	712			
◆	725	◆		╱†*
	725			╱▲
T	729			
⊙	744			
$	745			
▦	754			
✕	758			
♥	760			
✕	762			
�P	801			
▩	814			
▲	815			
∅	838			
✚	839			
★	840			
d	841			
▷	842			
	844	⌐		╱°
5	898	6		
▼	930			
∏	931			
♥	934			
H	935	◣		╱°
▨	936			
✕	937			
⊡	938			
◇	948			
◼	3021	◣		╱▲
❖	3031			
2	3032			╱†
∧	3033			
⊙	3047			
▦	3064			

X	DMC	¼X	B'ST	X
◼	3371	◣	╱	
2	3712			
O	3716	⊙		
8	3750			
◼	3781	◣		
✳	3782			
⊙	3787			
+	3790			
	3799		╱▲	
⊙	Mill Hill Bead - 02013			

☐ Blue area indicates first row of right section of design.

* Use 304 for drum. Use 356 for flesh.

† Use 414 for snow. Use 725 for lantern and windows.
Use 3032 for all other.

★ Use 2 strands of floss for windows.

▲ Use 1 strand of floss and 1 strand of Kreinik Cord Blending Filament - 002C.

° Use 844 for buildings. Use 935 for holly leaves.

△ Use 3021 for fur trim. Use 3799 for mountains.

STITCH COUNT (166w x 96h)

14 count	11⅞" x	6⅞"
16 count	10⅜" x	6"
18 count	9¼" x	5⅜"
22 count	7⅝" x	4⅜"

Christmas Journey in Frame (shown on pages 8-9): The design was stitched over 2 fabric threads on a 21" x 16" piece of Antique White Lugana (25 ct). Three strands of floss were used for Cross Stitch and 1 strand for Half Cross Stitch and Backstitch, unless otherwise noted in the color key. Attach beads using 1 strand of DMC 304 floss. See Attaching Beads, page 96. It was custom framed.

Needlework adaptation by Nancy Dockter.

NOEL NATURALS

#1 (42w x 41h)

#2 (42w x 42h)

Designs by Jorja Hernandez.

#5 (40w x 40h)

#6 (40w x 39h)

#9 (42w x 43h)

#10 (41w x 41h)

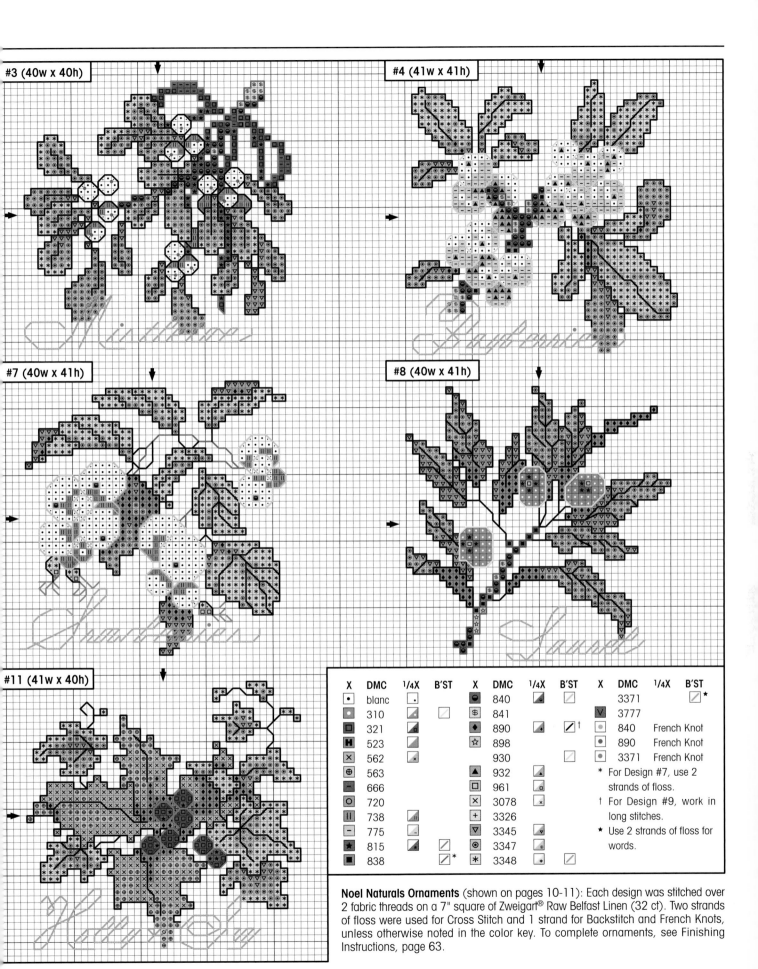

#3 (40w x 40h)

#4 (41w x 41h)

#7 (40w x 41h)

#8 (40w x 41h)

#11 (41w x 40h)

X	DMC	¼X	B'ST	X	DMC	¼X	B'ST	X	DMC	¼X	B'ST
●	blanc			◔	840				3371		★
⊙	310			$	841			▼	3777		
▣	321			◆	890		†		840	French Knot	
H	523			☆	898				890	French Knot	
✕	562				930				3371	French Knot	
⊕	563			▲	932						
⊖	666			▢	961			* For Design #7, use 2			
⦿	720			✕	3078			strands of floss.			
‖	738			+	3326			† For Design #9, work in			
—	775			▽	3345			long stitches.			
★	815			⦿	3347			★ Use 2 strands of floss for			
▪	838		*	✳	3348			words.			

Noel Naturals Ornaments (shown on pages 10-11): Each design was stitched over 2 fabric threads on a 7" square of Zweigart® Raw Belfast Linen (32 ct). Two strands of floss were used for Cross Stitch and 1 strand for Backstitch and French Knots, unless otherwise noted in the color key. To complete ornaments, see Finishing Instructions, page 63.

O COME, ALL YE FAITHFUL

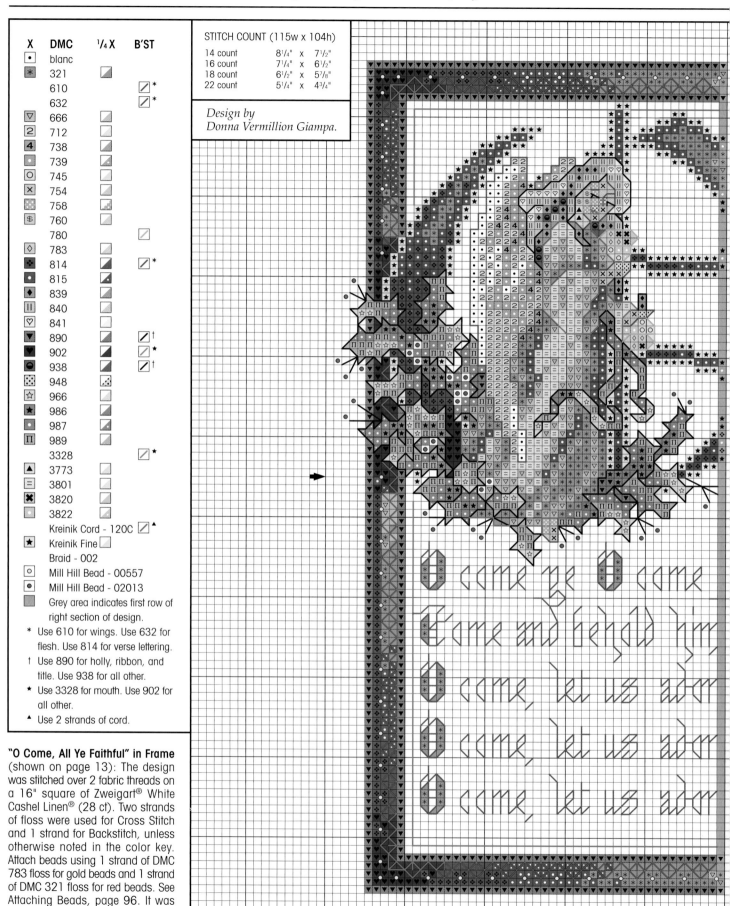

X	DMC	¼ X	B'ST
•	blanc		
✳	321	◢	
	610		◿ *
	632		◿ *
▽	666	◢	
2	712	◻	
4	738	◢	
	739	◢	
◻	745	◻	
✕	754	◢	
▦	758	◢	
$	760	◢	
	780		◿
❋	814	◢	◿ *
◙	815	◢	
◆	839	◢	
‖	840	◢	
♡	841	◻	
▼	890	◢	◿ †
◼	902	◢	◿ *
◖	938	◢	◿ †
▨	948	▨	
☆	966	◢	
★	986	◢	
◻	987	◢	
∏	989	◢	
	3328		◿ *
▲	3773	◻	
=	3801	◻	
✖	3820	◻	
◻	3822	◢	
	Kreinik Cord - 120C	◿ ▲	
★	Kreinik Fine	◻	
	Braid - 002		
◉	Mill Hill Bead - 00557		
●	Mill Hill Bead - 02013		
▦	Grey area indicates first row of right section of design.		

* Use 610 for wings. Use 632 for flesh. Use 814 for verse lettering.
† Use 890 for holly, ribbon, and title. Use 938 for all other.
★ Use 3328 for mouth. Use 902 for all other.
▲ Use 2 strands of cord.

STITCH COUNT (115w x 104h)

14 count	8¼"	x	7½"
16 count	7¼"	x	6½"
18 count	6½"	x	5⅞"
22 count	5¼"	x	4¾"

Design by Donna Vermillion Giampa.

"O Come, All Ye Faithful" in Frame (shown on page 13): The design was stitched over 2 fabric threads on a 16" square of Zweigart® White Cashel Linen® (28 ct). Two strands of floss were used for Cross Stitch and 1 strand for Backstitch, unless otherwise noted in the color key. Attach beads using 1 strand of DMC 783 floss for gold beads and 1 strand of DMC 321 floss for red beads. See Attaching Beads, page 96. It was custom framed.

O come, all ye faithful

The Sounds of Christmas Ornaments (shown on page 14): Designs #1, #3, #4, and #6 were each stitched over 2 fabric threads on an 8" square of Zweigart® Cream Cashel Linen® (28 ct). Two strands of floss were used for Cross Stitch and 1 strand for Backstitch and French Knots.

For each ornament, you will need an 8" square of Cream Cashel Linen® for backing, 22" length of $1/4$" dia. satin cord, and clear-drying craft glue. For Designs #1 and #4, you will also need two $3^1/_2$" squares of adhesive mounting board and two $3^1/_2$" squares of batting. For Designs #3 and #6 you will also need two $3^1/_2$" dia. circles of adhesive mounting board and two $3^1/_2$" dia. circles of batting.

Trim stitched piece $3/_4$" larger than design on all sides. Using stitched piece as a pattern, cut backing fabric the same size.

Remove paper from one mounting board piece and press one batting piece onto mounting board. Repeat with remaining mounting board and batting. Clip $1/_2$" into edge of stitched piece at $1/_2$" intervals. Center wrong side of stitched piece over batting on one mounting board piece; fold edges of stitched piece to back of mounting board and glue in place. For ornament back, repeat with backing fabric and remaining mounting board.

Referring to photo and beginning at top center of stitched piece, glue cord to edge of ornament. For hanger, extend cord and form a loop; glue ends of cord to wrong side of ornament front.

Matching wrong sides, glue ornament front and back together.

The Sounds of Christmas Pillows (shown on page 15): Designs #2 and #5 were each stitched over 2 fabric threads on a 12" square of Zweigart® Cream Lugana (25 ct). Three strands of floss were used for Cross Stitch and 1 strand for Backstitch.

For each pillow, you will need two 9" square pieces of fabric for pillow front and back, 36" length of $1/_4$" dia. purchased cording with attached seam allowance, 20" length of $3/_8$"w gold trim, fabric glue, and polyester fiberfill.

Note: Use $1/_2$" seam allowance for all seams.
Centering design, trim stitched piece to measure $4^3/_4$" square.

For pillow front, center stitched piece on one 9" square of fabric; pin in place. Using a zigzag stitch, machine sew stitched piece to fabric close to raw edges. Glue gold trim around outside edge of stitched piece, covering raw edges.

If needed, trim seam allowances of cording to $1/_2$". Matching raw edges and beginning at center of bottom edge, pin cording to right side of pillow front, making a $3/_8$" clip in seam allowances of cording at corners. Ends of cording should overlap approximately 4". Turn overlapped ends of cording toward outside edge of pillow front; baste cording to pillow front.

Matching right sides and raw edges, pin pillow front and backing fabric together. Leaving an opening for turning, use a $1/_2$" seam allowance to sew pillow front and backing fabric together. Trim seam allowances diagonally at corners; turn pillow right side out, carefully pushing corners outward. Stuff pillow with polyester fiberfill and blind stitch opening closed.

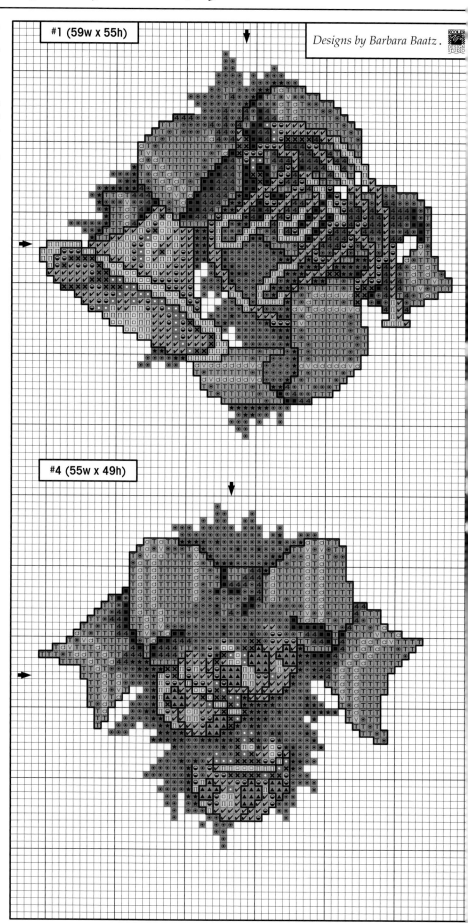

#1 (59w x 55h)

Designs by Barbara Baatz.

#4 (55w x 49h)

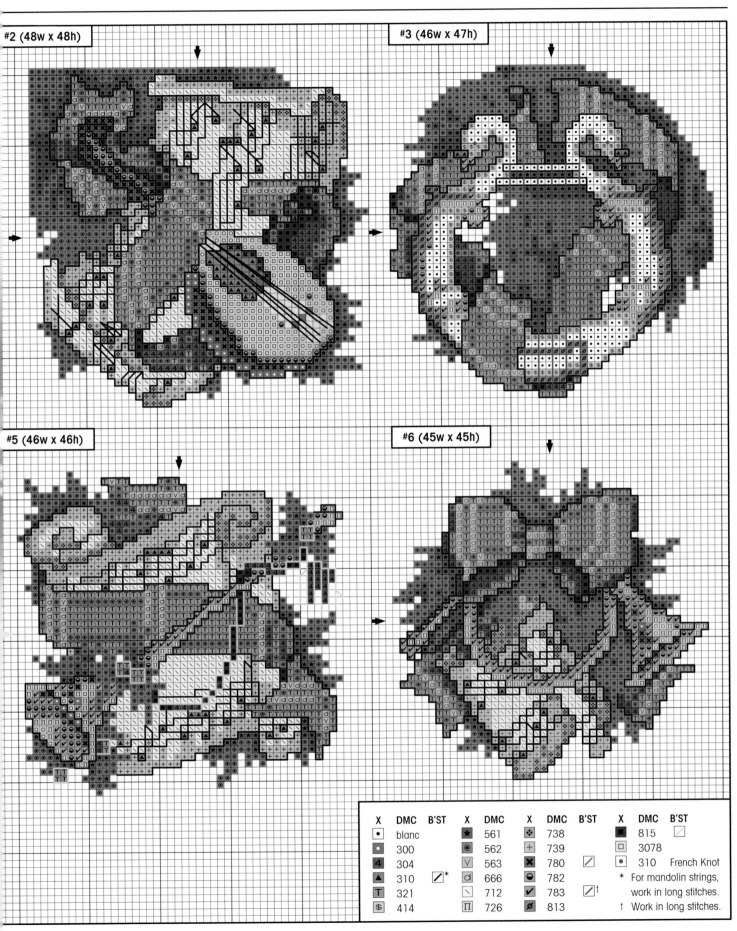

#2 (48w x 48h)

#3 (46w x 47h)

#5 (46w x 46h)

#6 (45w x 45h)

X	DMC	B'ST	X	DMC	X	DMC	B'ST	X	DMC	B'ST
•	blanc		★	561	❖	738		■	815	/
◉	300		◉	562	+	739		▣	3078	
4	304		V	563	✖	780	/	●	310	French Knot
▲	310	/*	d	666	◒	782				
T	321		\	712	✔	783	/†			
$	414		Π	726	∅	813				

* For mandolin strings,
work in long stitches.

† Work in long stitches.

55

WOODLAND SANTA

X	DMC	¼X	½X	B'ST	X	DMC	¼X	½X	B'ST
	blanc					754			
*	blanc					758			
	310					760			
4	318					762			
₵†	318 & 436				>†	762 & 822			
2	318 & 642					801			○
C	321					814			
X	341		L	★	~	822			
∩	413					839			
◆	414					840			
⊖†	414 & 640					841			
e	415					842			
✖†	415 & 644					869			
⊞	420				†	869 & 433			
▲†	420 & 434					902			
0	433					926			
X	434				(	927			
◆◆	435				♥	935		☆	
∽	436				▲	938			
a	437				••	948			
▲	498					986		⊠	
✓	503		—		3	988		∩	
H	504				○	989		↑	
	632					3064			
#	640		●		$	3328			▲
★	642		V		■	3371			▲
m	644		I		▲	3712			
■	666				?	3747		•|•	
T	676				+	3756			
↗	676 & 437				✛	3768			
=	677				⬆	3787		■	
⌐†	677 & 739				▦	3799			★
6	680				○	3801			
✖†	680 & 435				●	938	French Knot		
●	729								
△†	729 & 436								
n	738								
I	739								

Grey area indicates last row of previous section of design.

* Use 1 strand of floss and 1 strand of Kreinik Blending Filament - 032.

† Use 1 strand of each floss color listed.

★ Use 341 for snow. Use 3799 for all other.

○ For puppet's strings, use 2 strands of floss and work in long stitches.

▲ Use 3328 for Santa's mouth. Use 3371 for all other.

STITCH COUNT (168w x 248h)

14 count	12"	x	17¾"
16 count	10½"	x	15½"
18 count	9⅜"	x	13⅞"
22 count	7¾"	x	11⅜"

Woodland Santa Stocking (shown on page 17): The design was stitched over 2 fabric threads on a 19" x 24" piece of Zweigart® Raw Belfast Linen (32 ct). Two strands of floss were used for Cross Stitch and 1 strand for Half Cross Stitch, Backstitch, and French Knots. Personalize stocking using alphabet on page 62.

For stocking, you will need a 19" x 24" piece of fabric for backing, two 19" x 24" pieces of fabric for lining, 45" length of ¼" dia. purchased cording with attached seam allowance, 2" x 7" length of fabric for hanger, tracing paper, and fabric marking pencil.

Matching arrows of Stocking Pattern, page 62, to form one pattern, trace pattern onto tracing paper; add a ½" seam allowance on all sides and cut out pattern. Referring to photo for placement, position pattern on wrong side of stitched piece; pin pattern in place. Use fabric marking pencil to draw around pattern; remove pattern and cut out on drawn line. Use pattern and cut one from backing fabric and **two** from lining fabric.

If needed, trim seam allowance of cording to ½". Matching raw edges, baste cording to right side of stocking front.

Matching right sides and leaving top edge open, use a ½" seam allowance to sew stitched piece and backing fabric together. Clip seam allowance at curves and turn stocking right side out. Press top edge of stocking ½" to wrong side.

Matching right sides and leaving top edge open, use a ⅝" seam allowance to sew lining pieces together; trim seam allowance close to stitching. **Do not turn lining right side out.** Press top edge of lining ½" to wrong side.

For hanger, press each long edge of fabric strip ½" to center. Matching long edges, fold strip in half and sew close to folded edges. Matching short edges, fold hanger in half and whipstitch to inside of stocking at right seam.

With wrong sides facing, place lining inside stocking; blind stitch lining to stocking.

Design by Donna Vermillion Giampa.

57

WOODLAND SANTA

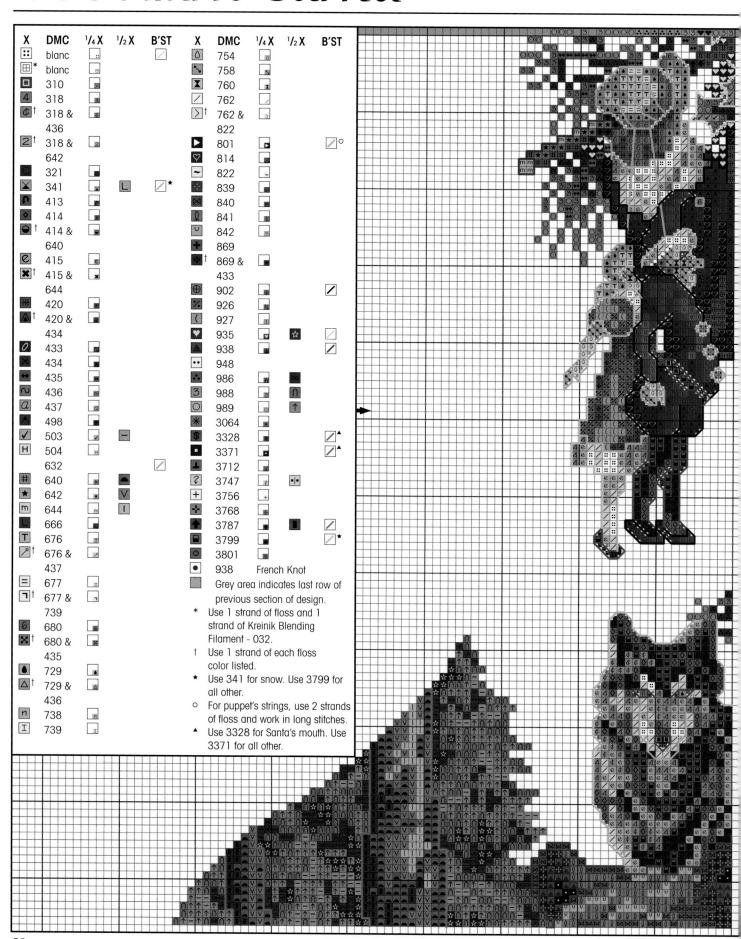

X	DMC	¼ X	½ X	B'ST		X	DMC	¼ X	½ X	B'ST
∷	blanc	∷		╱		◊	754	◊		
⊞*	blanc	⊞				◣	758	◣		
◻	310	◻				✕	760	✕		
4	318	4				╱	762	╱		
¢†	318 & 436	¢				⟩†	762 & 822	⟩		
2†	318 & 642	2				▶	801	▶		╱°
◻	321	◻				♥	814			
✕	341	x	L	╱*		~	822	~		
⋒	413	⋒				✚	839	✚		
◈	414	◈				⊠	840	⊠		
◉†	414 & 640	◉				◖	841	◖		
e	415	e				∪	842	∪		
✖†	415 & 644	✖				✚	869	✚		
▦	420	▦				✖†	869 & 433	✖		
▲†	420 & 434	▲				⊕	902	⊕		╱
0	433	0				⁒	926	⁒		
✕	434	✕				(	927	(		
◆◆	435	◆◆				♥	935	♥	☆	╱
∿	436	∿				▲	938	▲		╱
α	437	α				••	948			
▲	498	▲				✱	986	✱	◼	
✓	503	✓	—			3	988	3	∩	
H	504	H				○	989	○	↑	
	632		╱			✳	3064	✳		
▦	640	▦	◠			$	3328	$		╱▲
★	642	★	V			◼	3371	◼		╱▲
m	644	m	I			?	3712	?		
◼	666	◼				🔊	3747	🔊	•⊡	
T	676	T				+	3756	+		
◢†	676 & 437	◢				✦	3768			
=	677	=				▲	3787	▲	▮	╱
⌐†	677 & 739	⌐				◼	3799	◼		╱*
6	680	6				○	3801	○		
✖†	680 & 435	✖				●	938	French Knot		
◖	729	◖				▨	Grey area indicates last row of previous section of design.			
△†	729 & 436	△								
n	738	n								
I	739	I								

* Use 1 strand of floss and 1 strand of Kreinik Blending Filament - 032.

† Use 1 strand of each floss color listed.

★ Use 341 for snow. Use 3799 for all other.

° For puppet's strings, use 2 strands of floss and work in long stitches.

▲ Use 3328 for Santa's mouth. Use 3371 for all other.

WOODLAND SANTA

X	DMC	1/4 X	1/2 X	B'ST
∷	blanc	∷		/
⊞*	blanc	⊞		
◘	310	◘		
4	318	4		
¢†	318 & 436	¢		
2†	318 & 642	2		
C	321	C		
⧗	341	⧗	L	/★
∩	413	∩		
◊	414	◊		

X	DMC	1/4 X
◓†	414 & 640	◓
e	415	e
✖†	415 & 644	✖
⧻	420	⧻
▲†	420 & 434	▲
0	433	0
X	434	X
◆◆	435	◆◆
∾	436	∾

X	DMC	1/4 X	1/2 X	B'ST
a	437	a		
∧	498	∧		
√	503	√	–	
H	504	H		
	632			/
#	640	#	◓	
★	642	★	V	
m	644	m	I	
L	666	L		
T	676	T		
⁄†	676 & 437	⁄		

X	DMC	1/4 X
=	677	=
┐†	677 & 739	┐
6	680	6
⤧†	680 & 435	⤧
●	729	●
△†	729 & 436	△
n	738	n
I	739	I
0	754	0

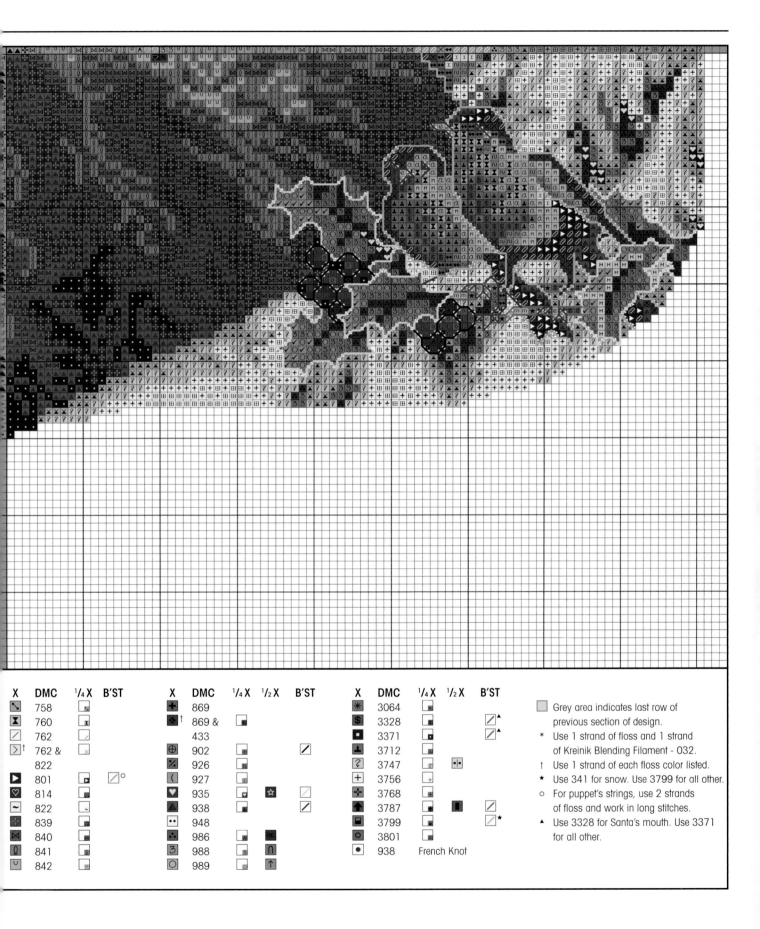

X	DMC	¼ X	B'ST		X	DMC	¼ X	½ X	B'ST		X	DMC	¼ X	½ X	B'ST
◣	758	◣			✚	869					✳	3064			
✕	760	✕			❋†	869 &					$	3328			╱▲
╱	762	╱				433					▣	3371			╱▲
▷†	762 &	▷			⊕	902			╱		⊥	3712			
	822				⁒	926					?	3747		••	
▶	801	▶	╱°		⦅	927					✚	3756			
♡	814				♥	935		☆	╱		✦	3768			
∼	822				▲	938			╱		↑	3787		▮	╱
⋈	839				••	948					▪	3799			╱★
◐	840				⁛	986		⊠			○	3801			
▯	841				3	988		∩			●	938	French Knot		
∪	842				○	989		↑							

☐ Grey area indicates last row of previous section of design.

* Use 1 strand of floss and 1 strand of Kreinik Blending Filament - 032.

† Use 1 strand of each floss color listed.

★ Use 341 for snow. Use 3799 for all other.

○ For puppet's strings, use 2 strands of floss and work in long stitches.

▲ Use 3328 for Santa's mouth. Use 3371 for all other.

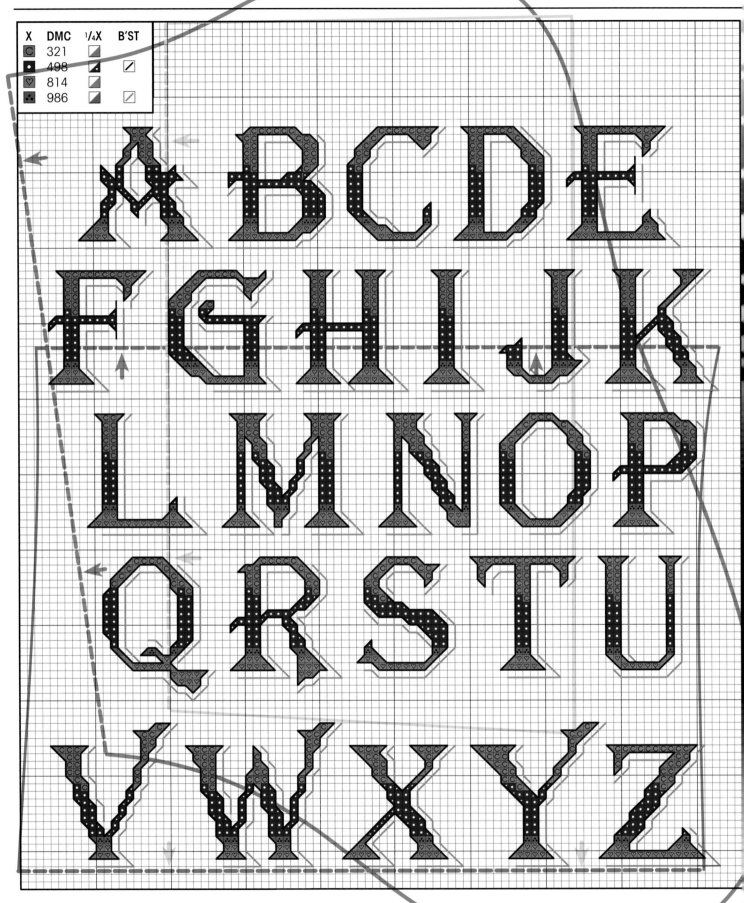

X	DMC	1/4X	B'ST
	321		
	498		
	814		
	986		

MERRIE ALPHABET

Merrie Alphabet in Frame (shown on page 19, chart on pages 64-69): The design was stitched over 2 fabric threads on a 21" x 29" piece of Zweigart® Platinum Cashel Linen® (28 ct). Two strands of floss were used for Cross Stitch and 1 strand for Backstitch and French Knots, unless otherwise noted in the color key. Attach beads using 1 strand of DMC 321 floss. See Attaching Beads, page 96. It was custom framed.

Santa Shaker Box (shown on page 20, chart on pages 67 and 69): The letter "S" and the Santa were stitched over 2 fabric threads on an 8" square of Zweigart® Platinum Cashel Linen® (28 ct). Two strands of floss were used for Cross Stitch and 1 strand for Backstitch.

For Shaker box, you will need a 4" dia. Shaker box, 4" dia. circle of batting for lid, 13½" x 2½" piece of fabric for box bottom, 13½" length of ¼"w braid, tracing paper, pencil, fabric marking pencil, and clear-drying craft glue.

For pattern, trace around box lid onto tracing paper; add ¾" on all sides and cut out. Center pattern on wrong side of stitched piece; pin pattern in place. Use a fabric marking pencil to draw around pattern; remove pattern and cut out on drawn line. Clip ¼" into edge of stitched piece at 1" intervals. Glue batting on top of lid. Centering wrong side of stitched piece on batting, fold edges of stitched piece down and glue to side of lid. Referring to photo, glue braid to side of lid.

For box bottom, press fabric piece under ½" on short edges and ¼" on one long edge. Placing folded edge along bottom edge of box, glue fabric to box. Fold top edge of fabric to inside of box and glue in place.

Cardinal in Frame (shown on page 20, chart on pages 64-65): The letter "C" and the cardinal were stitched over 2 fabric threads on an 8" square of Zweigart® Antique White Lugana (25 ct). Three strands of floss were used for Cross Stitch and 1 strand for Backstitch and French Knots. It was custom framed.

Yuletide Ornaments (shown on pages 20-21, charts on pages 64 and 66-69): Portions of the design (refer to photo) were each stitched over 2 fabric threads on an 8" square of Zweigart® Antique White Lugana (25 ct). Three strands of floss were used for Cross Stitch and 1 strand for Backstitch and French Knots. For floss blended with blending filament, use 3 strands of floss and 1 strand of blending filament. Attach beads using 1 strand of DMC 321 floss. See Attaching Beads, page 96.

For each ornament, you will need a 6" square of Antique White Lugana for backing, 5" x 9" piece of adhesive mounting board, tracing paper, pencil, 5" x 9" piece of batting, 15" length of ¼" dia. purchased cord, and clear-drying craft glue.

For pattern, fold tracing paper in half and place fold on dashed line of desired pattern; trace pattern onto tracing paper. Cut out pattern; unfold and press flat. Draw around pattern twice on mounting board and twice on batting; cut out. Remove paper from one piece of mounting board and press one batting piece onto mounting board. Repeat with remaining mounting board and batting.

Referring to photo, position pattern on wrong side of stitched piece; pin pattern in place. Cut stitched piece 1" larger than pattern on all sides. Cut backing fabric same size as stitched piece. Clip ½" into edge of stitched piece at ½" intervals. Center wrong side of stitched piece over batting on one mounting board piece; fold edges of stitched piece to back of mounting board and glue in place. For ornament back, repeat with backing fabric and remaining mounting board. Matching wrong sides, glue ornament front and back together.

Beginning and ending at bottom center of ornament, glue cord to side of ornament, overlapping ends of cord.

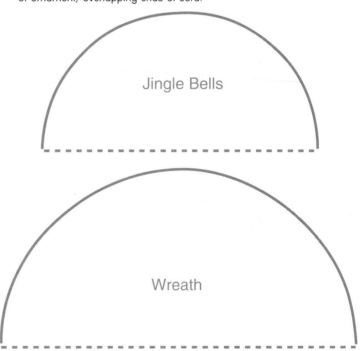

Angel
Ornaments

Jingle Bells

Virgin Mary and Child
Christmas Tree

Wreath

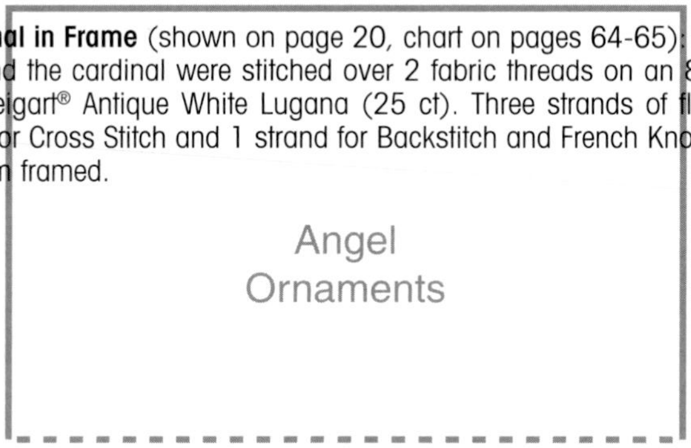

FINISHING INSTRUCTIONS

Noel Naturals Ornaments (shown on pages 10-11, charts on pages 50-51):

For each ornament, you will need a 5" square of fabric for backing, two 3½" square pieces of adhesive mounting board, two 3½" square pieces of batting, 17" length of ¼" dia. purchased cording with attached seam allowance, 6" length of ⅜"w grosgrain ribbon for hanger, and clear-drying craft glue.

Centering design, trim stitched piece to measure 5" square.

Remove paper from one piece of mounting board and press one batting piece onto mounting board. Repeat with remaining mounting board and batting piece.

Center stitched piece over batting on one mounting board piece; fold edges of stitched piece to back of mounting board and glue in place. For ornament back, repeat with backing fabric and remaining mounting board.

Beginning and ending at bottom center of stitched piece, glue cording seam allowance to wrong side of ornament front, overlapping ends of cording.

For hanger, fold ribbon in half and glue ends to top center of ornament front on wrong side. Matching wrong sides, glue ornament front and back together.

MERRIE ALPHABET

180w x 290h

Design by Donna Vermillion Giampa.

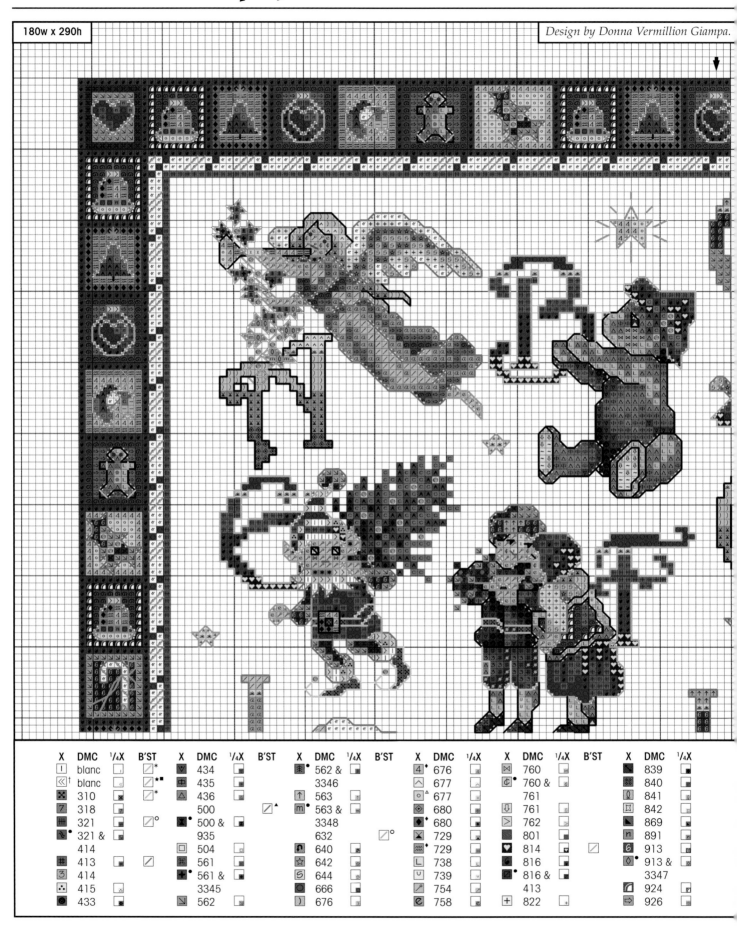

X	DMC	¼X	B'ST	X	DMC	¼X	B'ST	X	DMC	¼X	B'ST	X	DMC	¼X	X	DMC	¼X	B'ST	X	DMC	¼X
	blanc		*		434				562 &				676			760				839	
	blanc		★■		435				3346				677			760 &				840	
	310		*		436				563				677			761				841	
	318				500		▲		563 &				680			761				842	
	321		°		500 &				3348				680			762				869	
	321 &				935				632		°		729			801				891	
	414				504				640				729			814				913	
	413				561				642				738			816				913 &	
	414				561 &				644				739			816 &				3347	
	415				3345				666				754			413				924	
	433				562				676				758			822				926	

64

All project information on page 63.

X	DMC	¼X	B'ST	X	DMC	¼X	B'ST
a	927	a		✤	3712		
╱	928			~	3713		
■	935		╱☆	◗	3768		
▲	938		╱	●	3799		
I	948			✥	5282		╱
✳	3064			○	blanc	French Knot	
▶	3328		╱	●	666	French Knot	
◆	3345			●	938	French Knot	
▲	3346			○	3347	French Knot	
C	3347			○	5282	French Knot	
–	3348			◎	Mill Hill Bead - 00165		

◻ Grey area indicates last row of previous section of design.

* Use blanc for gingerbread men. Use 310 for all other.
† Use 2 strands of floss and 1 strand of Kreinik Blending Filament – 032.
✦ Use 1 strand of floss and 1 strand of Kreinik Blending Filament – 032.
▪ Work in long stitches.
○ Use 632 for flesh. Use 321 for all other.

• For linen, use 1 strand of each floss color listed. For Lugana, use 2 strands of first floss color listed and 1 strand of second floss color listed.
▲ For pine needles, use 2 strands of floss.
• Use 2 strands of floss and 1 strand of Kreinik Blending Filament – 002.
△ Use 2 strands of floss and 1 strand of Kreinik Blending Filament – 091.
☆ For mistletoe branches, use 2 strands of floss.

X	DMC	¼X	B'ST	X	DMC	¼X	B'ST	X	DMC	¼X	B'ST	X	DMC	¼X	X	DMC	¼X	B'ST	X	DMC	¼X
I	blanc		⁄*	V	434			*	562 &			4	676		⋈	760			◼	839	
≪†	blanc	≪	⁄·■	⊞	435				3346			∧	677		ℭ·	760 &			⊠	840	
✕	310	✕	⁄*	△	436			↑	563			○△	677			761			◖	841	
7	318				500		⁄▲	m	563 &			◇	680		⇩	761			⋈	842	
⊞	321		⁄°	✕	500 &				3348			◆	680		▷	762			◣	869	
◣·	321 &				935				632		⁄°	✕	729			801			n	891	
	414			□	504			n	640			⊠·	729		❤	814		⁄	6	913	
⊞	413		⁄	⊞	561			☆	642			L	738		◼	816			◊	913 &	
3	414			✚·	561 &			5	644			┘	739		◼·	816 &				3347	
∴	415				3345			◼	666			⁄	754			413			⊡	924	
◉	433			⊠	562			)	676			ℯ	758		✚	822		⇨	926	

X	DMC	¼X	B'ST	X	DMC	¼X	B'ST
a	927	a		✦	3712		
╱	928			~	3713		
●	935		╱☆	⟲	3768		
▲	938		╱	◪	3799		
I	948			✿	5282		╱
✳	3064			○	blanc	French Knot	
►	3328		╱	●	666	French Knot	
▲	3345			●	938	French Knot	
△	3346			●	3347	French Knot	
C	3347			○	5282	French Knot	
─	3348			◎	Mill Hill Bead – 00165		

Grey area indicates last row of previous section of design.

* Use blanc for gingerbread men. Use 310 for all other.
† Use 2 strands of floss and 1 strand of Kreinik Blending Filament – 032.
★ Use 1 strand of floss and 1 strand of Kreinik Blending Filament – 032.
▪ Work in long stitches.
○ Use 632 for flesh. Use 321 for all other.

• For linen, use 1 strand of each floss color listed. For Lugana, use 2 strands of first floss color listed and 1 strand of second floss color listed.
▲ For pine needles, use 2 strands of floss.
• Use 2 strands of floss and 1 strand of Kreinik Blending Filament – 002.
▲ Use 2 strands of floss and 1 strand of Kreinik Blending Filament – 091.
☆ For mistletoe branches, use 2 strands of floss.

MERRIE ALPHABET

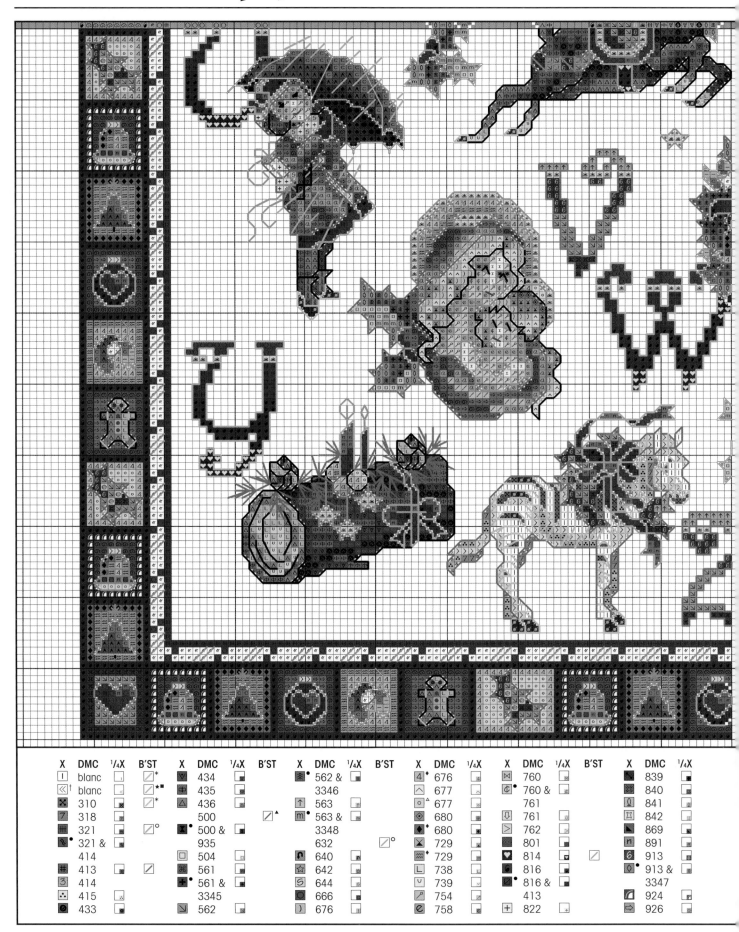

X	DMC	¼X	B'ST	X	DMC	¼X	B'ST	X	DMC	¼X	B'ST	X	DMC	¼X	X	DMC	¼X	B'ST	X	DMC	¼X
	blanc		⁄*	⊎	434			•	562 &			◆	676		⊠	760			◼	839	
	blanc		⁄★◼	⊞	435				3346				677		¢•	760 &				840	
✕	310		⁄*	△	436			↑	563			○	677			761				841	
	318				500		⁄▲	m•	563 &			◇	680		⇓	761				842	
⊞	321		⁄°	✕	500 &				3348			◆	680		⊳	762			◣	869	
•	321 &				935				632		⁄°	✕	729			801				891	
	414				504			∩	640			※◆	729		♥	814		⁄	6	913	
	413		⁄	⌗	561			☆	642			L	738		◆	816		•	913 &	
³	414			✚	561 &			S	644				739			816 &				3347	
•	415				3345				666				754				413			924	
◕	433				562				676				758		✛	822			926	

68

X	DMC	¼X	B'ST	X	DMC	¼X	B'ST
a	927	a		❖	3712		
/	928			~	3713		
●	935		☆	◗	3768		
▲	938		/	◼	3799		
I	948			⬇	5282		/
✳	3064		/	◦	blanc		French Knot
►	3328		/	●	666		French Knot
◄	3345			●	938		French Knot
▲	3346			●	3347		French Knot
C	3347			●	5282		French Knot
−	3348			◉	Mill Hill Bead - 00165		

☐ Grey area indicates last row of previous section of design.

* Use blanc for gingerbread men. Use 310 for all other.

† Use 2 strands of floss and 1 strand of Kreinik Blending Filament – 032.

* Use 1 strand of floss and 1 strand of Kreinik Blending Filament – 032.

■ Work in long stitches.

○ Use 632 for flesh. Use 321 for all other.

• For linen, use 1 strand of each floss color listed. For Lugana, use 2 strands of first floss color listed and 1 strand of second floss color listed.

▲ For pine needles, use 2 strands of floss.

• Use 2 strands of floss and 1 strand of Kreinik Blending Filament – 002.

▲ Use 2 strands of floss and 1 strand of Kreinik Blending Filament – 091.

☆ For mistletoe branches, use 2 strands of floss.

home sweet home

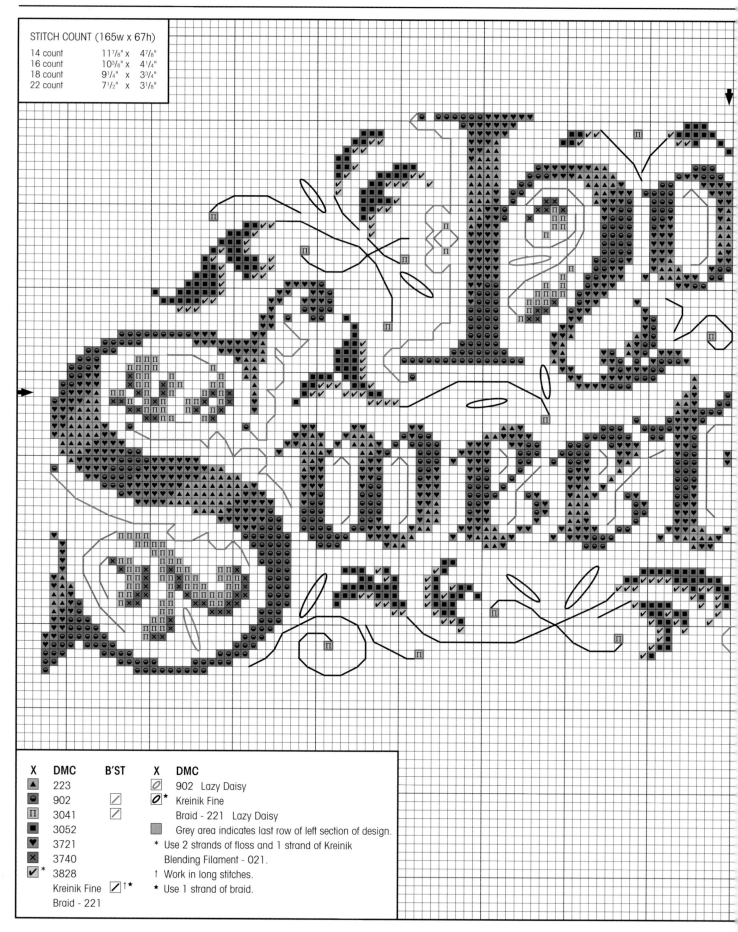

STITCH COUNT (165w x 67h)

count	width		height
14 count	11⁷/₈"	x	4⁷/₈"
16 count	10³/₈"	x	4¹/₄"
18 count	9¹/₄"	x	3³/₄"
22 count	7¹/₂"	x	3¹/₈"

X	DMC	B'ST	X	DMC
▲	223		⊘	902 Lazy Daisy
☻	902	∕	⊘*	Kreinik Fine
π	3041	∕		Braid - 221 Lazy Daisy
■	3052			Grey area indicates last row of left section of design.
♥	3721		*	Use 2 strands of floss and 1 strand of Kreinik
✕	3740			Blending Filament - 021.
✔*	3828		†	Work in long stitches.
	Kreinik Fine	∕†★	★	Use 1 strand of braid.
	Braid - 221			

"Home Sweet Home" Pillow (shown on pages 22-23): The design was stitched over 2 fabric threads on a 14" x 36" piece of Light Sand Edinborough Linen (36 ct). Two strands of floss were used for Cross Stitch and 1 for Backstitch and Lazy Daisy Stitches, unless otherwise noted in the color key.

For pillow, you will need two 23" x 19" pieces of fabric for pillow front and back and polyester fiberfill.

Centering design, trim stitched piece to measure 11" x 34".

Note: Use a 1/2" seam allowance for all seams.

For band, matching right sides and long edges, fold stitched piece in half; sew long edges together. Turn stitched piece right side out. With seam centered in back, press stitched piece flat. Matching right sides and

short edges, sew short edges together. Press seam open and turn band right side out.

For pillow, match right sides and raw edges of pillow front and back. Leaving an opening for turning, sew fabric pieces together; trim seam allowances diagonally at corners. Turn pillow right side out, carefully pushing corners outward; stuff pillow lightly with polyester fiberfill and blind stitch opening closed.

Referring to photo, place band around pillow.

Design by Sandy Orton.

GLORY OF THE LORD

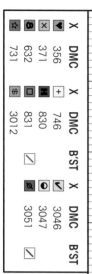

X					DMC
☆	⦿	✕	◀		356
					371
					632
					731

X					DMC
⊞	⬚	✖	+		746
					830
					831
					3012

B'ST			
◥			

X			DMC
◐	◑	◣	3046
			3047
			3051

B'ST
◥

"Glory of the Lord" Sampler in Frame (shown on pages 24-25): The design was stitched over 2 fabric threads on a 17" x 14" piece of Charles Craft, Inc®. Tea-Dyed Irish Linen (28 ct). Two strands of floss were used for Cross Stitch and 1 strand for Backstitch. Personalize and date design using DMC 632 floss and alphabet and numerals, page 74. It was custom framed.

Design by Mary Beale.

center initial

center date

center initial

center date

#1 (37w x 51h)

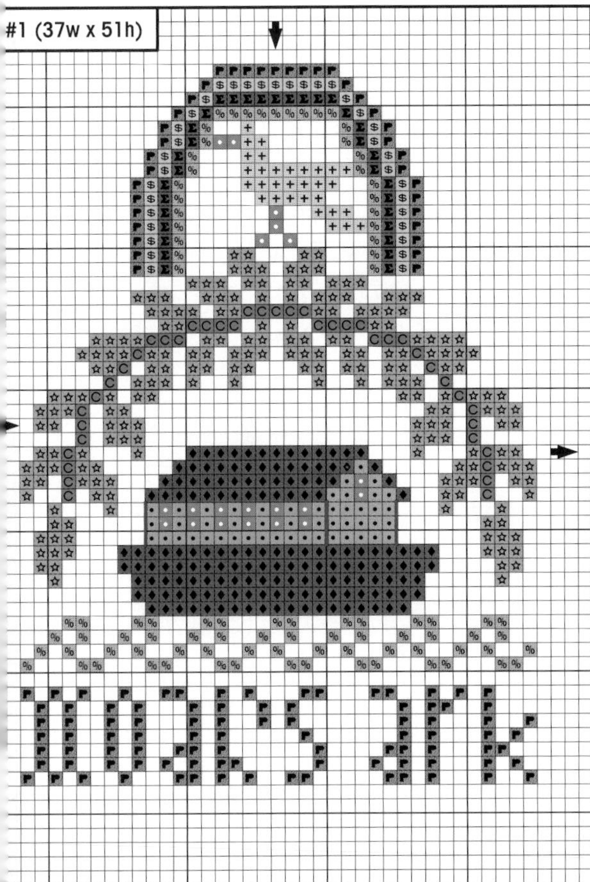

#2 (43w x 55h)

X	DMC	B'ST
◤	355	
2	356	
▽	407	
•	413	
T	420	
×	422	
◆	433	/
■	632	
Σ	730	
☆	731	
O	732	
•	780	
$	781	
Δ	831	
d	838	/
♥	844	
◒	924	
%	926	/
8	935	
C	937	
⊙	3012	
✱	3021	
+	3024	
H	3031	/
⊥	3046	
ø	3047	
✖	3051	

#3 (53w x 54h)

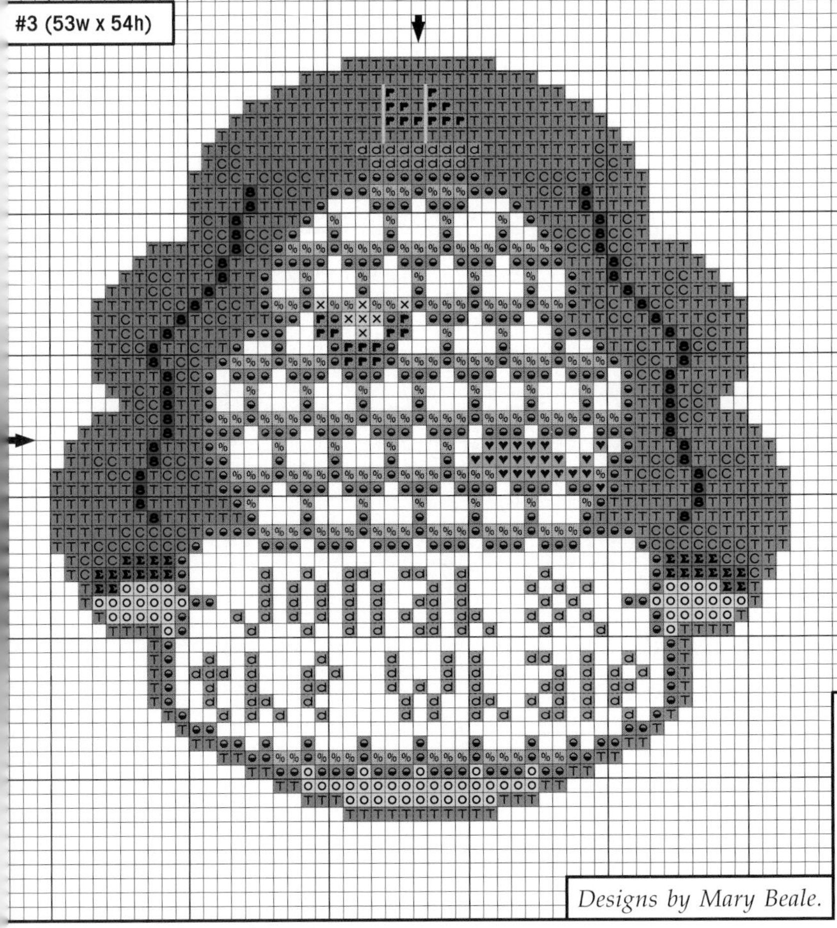

#4 (27w x 37h)

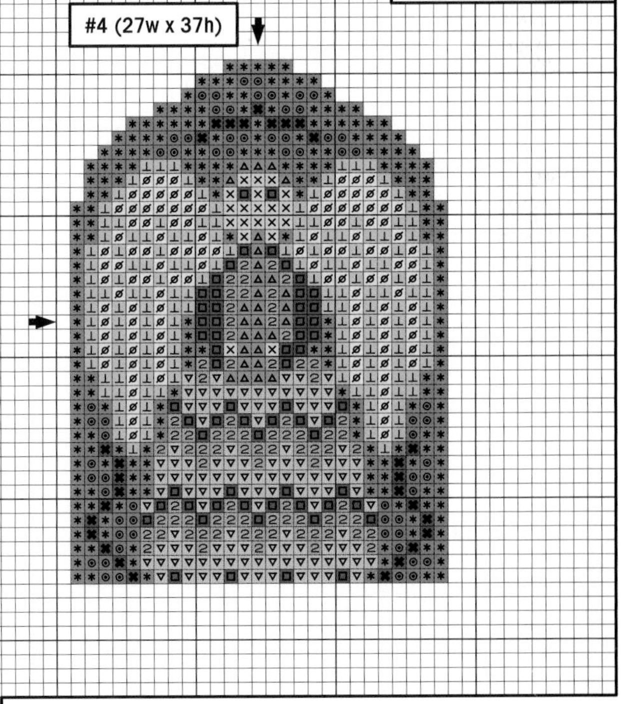

Angel Ornament (shown on page 26) **and Old Testament Ornaments** (shown on page 27): The designs were each stitched over 2 fabric threads on a 9" square of Unbleached Linen (27 ct). Two strands of floss were used for Cross Stitch and 1 strand for Backstitch. To complete ornaments, see Finishing Instructions, page 85.

Designs by Mary Beale.

GLORY OF THE LORD

Design by Mary Beale.

STITCH COUNT (97w x 101h)

14 count	7"	x 7¼"
16 count	6⅛"	x 6⅜"
18 count	5½"	x 5⅝"
22 count	4½"	x 4⅝"

center initials

center date

X	DMC	B'ST	X	DMC	B'ST
2	355		Σ	924	/
O	356	/	★	926	
\	407		▲	927	
×	422		+	928	
■	780		◉	935	
T	781		₱	937	
V	829		=	948	
♥	830		⊠	3031	
◉	895		✓	3345	

"Hark! The Herald Angels Sing" Pillow (shown on page 26): The design was stitched over 2 fabric threads on a 16" square of Unbleached Linen (27 ct). Two strands of floss were used for Cross Stitch and 1 strand for Backstitch. Personalize and date design using alphabet and numerals provided. To complete pillow, see Finishing Instructions, page 85.

fESTIVE TREE

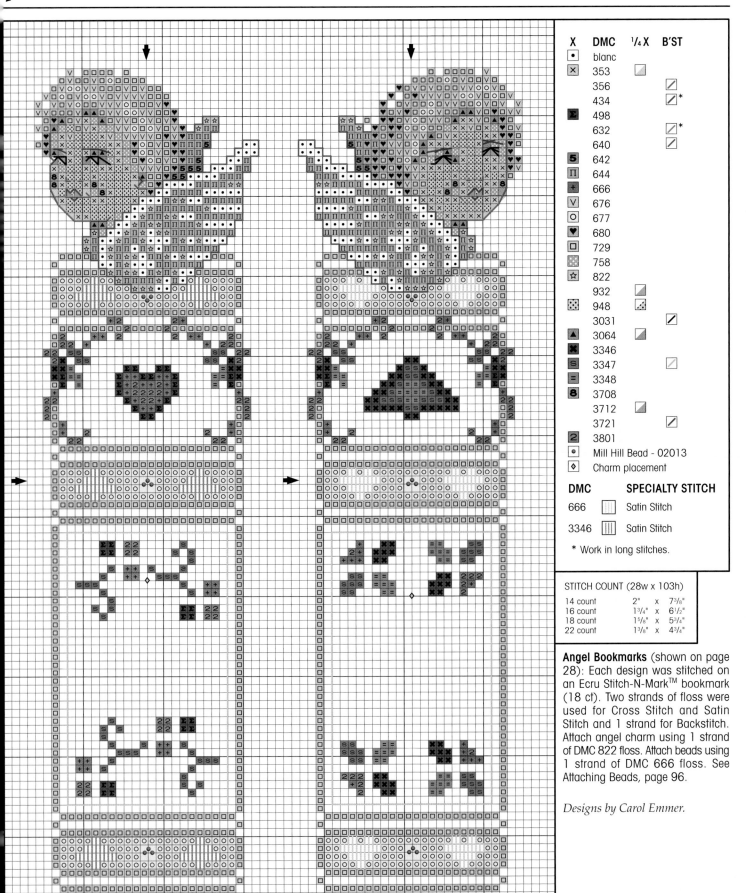

X	DMC	¼ X	B'ST
•	blanc	◩	
✗	353	◩	
	356		◿
	434		◿ *
◼	498		
	632		◿ *
	640		◿
5	642		
Π	644		
+	666		
V	676		
O	677		
♥	680		
□	729		
▧	758		
☆	822		
	932	◿	
▨	948	◪	
	3031		◿
▲	3064	◿	
✖	3346		
S	3347		◿
=	3348		
8	3708		
	3712	◩	
	3721		◿
2	3801		
⊙	Mill Hill Bead - 02013		
◇	Charm placement		

DMC	SPECIALTY STITCH	
666	▥	Satin Stitch
3346	▥	Satin Stitch

* Work in long stitches.

STITCH COUNT (28w x 103h)

14 count	2"	x	7³⁄₈"
16 count	1³⁄₄"	x	6¹⁄₂"
18 count	1⁵⁄₈"	x	5³⁄₄"
22 count	1³⁄₈"	x	4³⁄₄"

Angel Bookmarks (shown on page 28): Each design was stitched on an Ecru Stitch-N-Mark™ bookmark (18 ct). Two strands of floss were used for Cross Stitch and Satin Stitch and 1 strand for Backstitch. Attach angel charm using 1 strand of DMC 822 floss. Attach beads using 1 strand of DMC 666 floss. See Attaching Beads, page 96.

Designs by Carol Emmer.

FESTIVE TREE

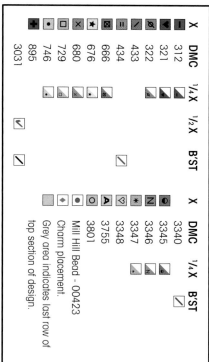

Festive Tree in Frame (shown on page 29): The design was stitched on a 15" x 17" piece of Antique White Aida (14 ct). Two strands of floss were used for Cross Stitch and 1 strand for Half Cross Stitch and Backstitch. Attach beads using 1 strand of DMC 3340 floss. See Attaching Beads, page 96. Attach charm using 1 strand of DMC 746 floss. It was custom framed.

For bead garlands, you will need Mill Hill Beads - 02013. Referring to photo for placement and using 1 strand of DMC 321 floss, bring needle up at ◆ symbol on chart; string beads. Take needle down at ◆ symbol; repeat for remaining garlands.

Design by Carol Emmer.

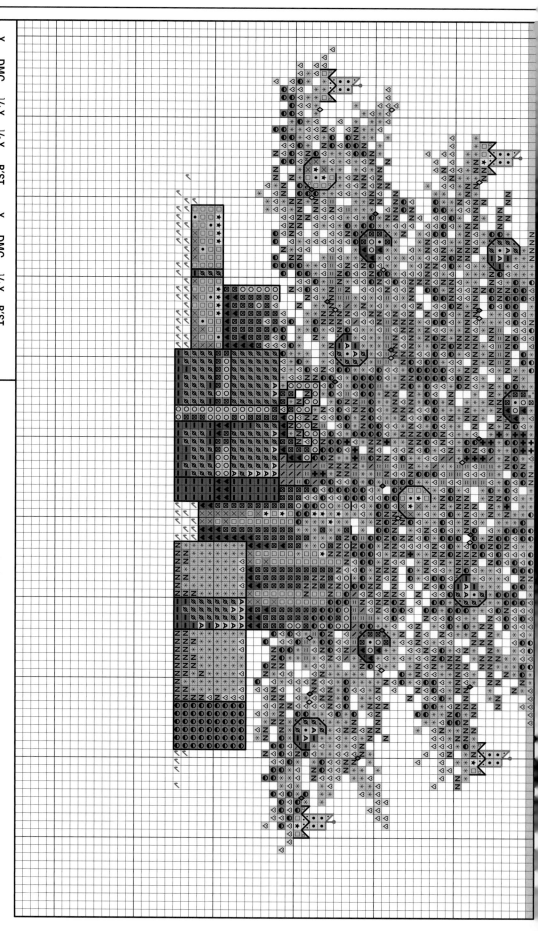

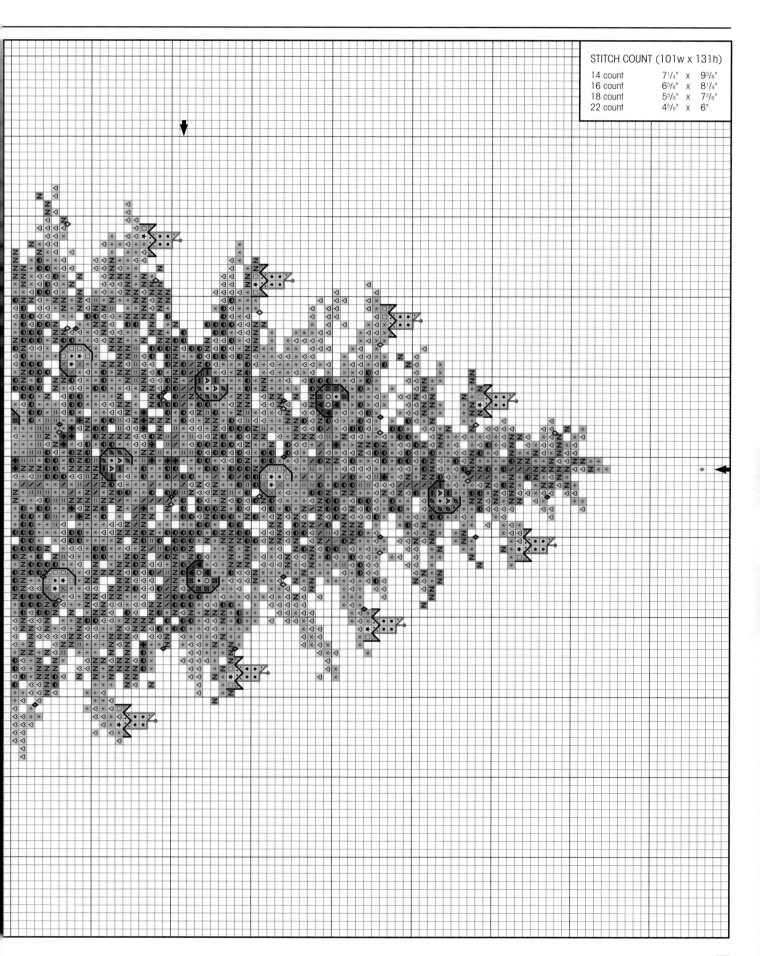

STITCH COUNT (101w x 131h)

14 count	7¼"	x 9⅜"
16 count	6⅜"	x 8¼"
18 count	5⅝"	x 7⅜"
22 count	4⅝"	x 6"

chorus of angels

X	DMC	¼X	B'ST	X	DMC	¼X	B'ST
⊥	blanc	⊥		~	928		
L	211			◖	935		
$	315			*	938		/*
6	316			◤	3041		
⊕	407			5	3042		
◇	420			○	3045		
T	433		/	T	3046		
+	435			/	3047		
3	436			□	3078		
◊	437				3328		/*
◆	520			%	3363		
m	523			◼	3712		
✓	524			#	3726		
	632		/*	◢	3727		
∅	640			◈	3740		□
Ⅲ	642			)	3743		
n	644			∩	3768		
↑	725			◖	3772		
=	727			✗	3773		
	738			:	3774		
♡	760			▲	3787		/
√	761			◿	5282		/*
↔	778			●	3768	French Knot	
6	781						
4	783						
◣	801						
<	822						
➡	869		/†				
♥	902		/				
0	924		/				
H	926						
Z	927						

◼ Blue area indicates last row of previous section of design.

* Use 632 for flesh. Use 938 for all other.

† For lantern strings, work in long stitches.

* Use 3328 for mouths. Use 5282 for all other.

Design by Donna Vermillion Giampa.

STITCH COUNT (250w x 237h)

14 count	17⅞"	x	17"
16 count	15⅝"	x	14⅞"
18 count	14"	x	13¼"
22 count	11⅜"	x	10⅞"

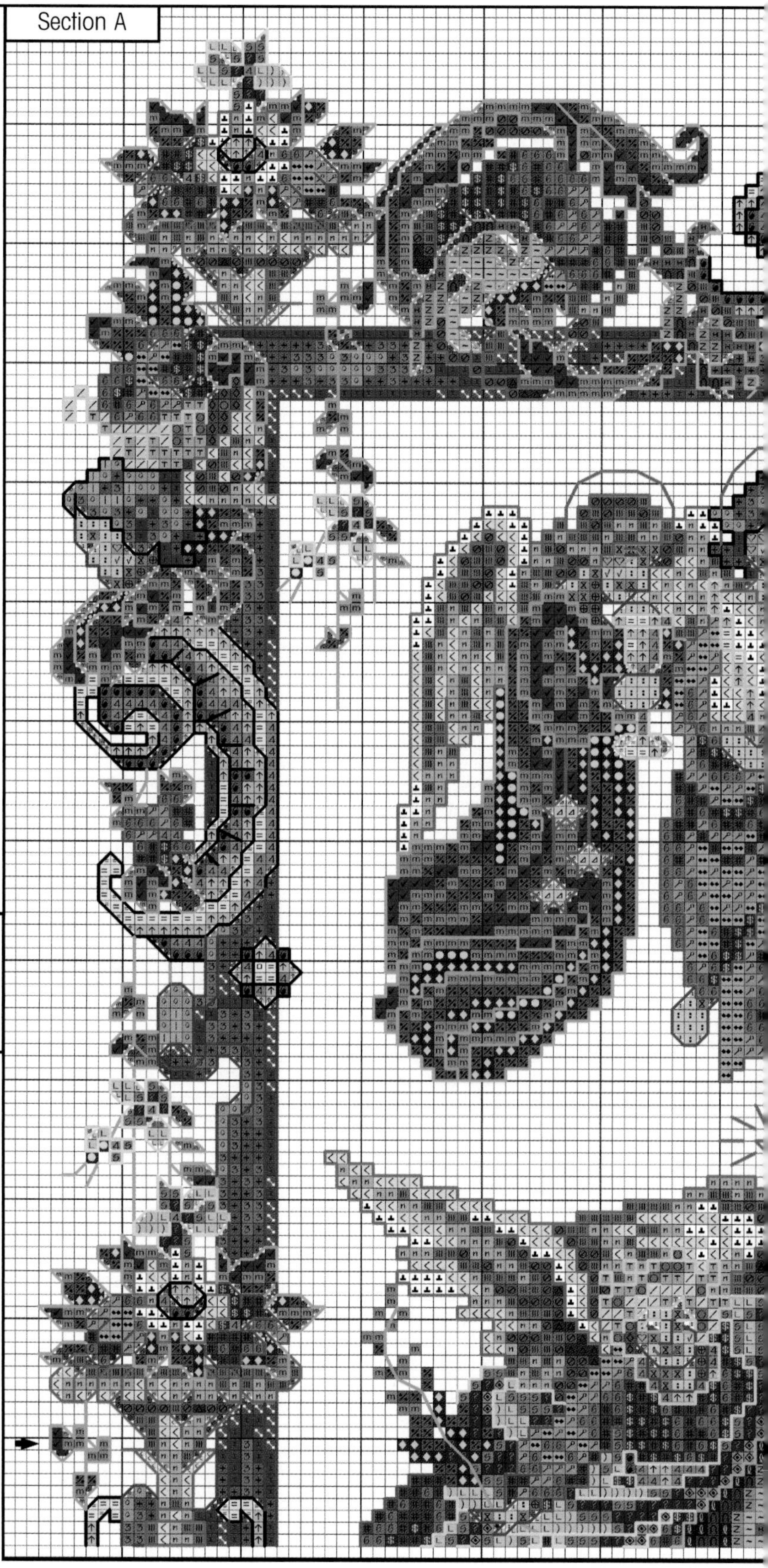

Note: The chart is divided into Sections A-F on pages 78-83. Refer to Diagram, page 83, for placement of design sections. We recommend stitching the design in alphabetical order by section.

Chorus of Angels in Frame (shown on page 31): The design was stitched on a 26" x 25" piece of Antique White Aida (14 ct). Two strands of floss were used for Cross Stitch and 1 strand for Backstitch and French Knots. It was custom framed.

Angels in Frame (shown on page 33): A portion of the design (refer to photo) was stitched over 2 fabric threads on a 13" square of Zweigart® Cream Cashel Linen® (28 ct). Two strands of floss were used for Cross Stitch and 1 strand for Backstitch. It was custom framed.

Chorus of Angels Pillow (shown on page 32): A portion of the design (refer to photo) was stitched over 2 fabric threads on a 14" x 13" piece of Zweigart® Cream Lugana (25 ct). Three strands of floss were used for Cross Stitch and 1 strand for Backstitch. To complete pillow, see Finishing Instructions, page 84.

Continued on page 81.

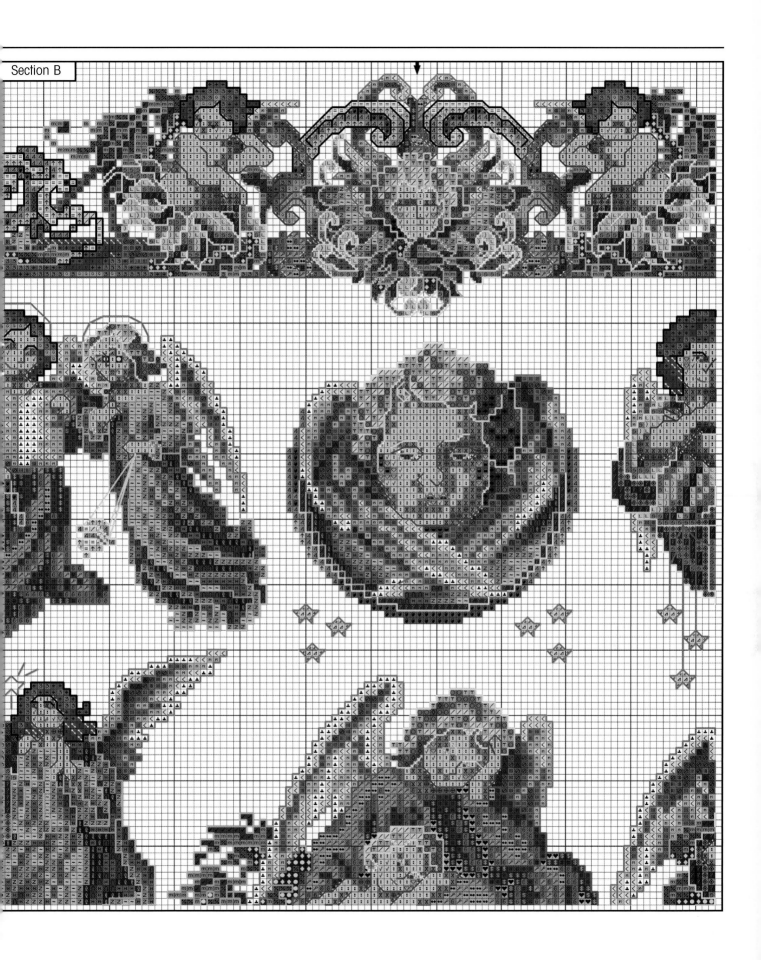

Section C

X	DMC	1/4X	B'ST
⊥	blanc	⊥	
L	211	L	
$	315	$	
6	316	6	
⊕	407		
◇	420		
I	433		╱
✚	435	*	
3	436		
∩	437		
◆	520		
m	523	m	
✔	524		
	632		╱*
∅	640		
Ⅲ	642		
n	644	n	
↑	725	↑	
=	727	=	
‖	738		
♡	760		
√	761		
◆◆	778		
6	781		
4	783	4	
◣	801		
<	822	<	
➡	869		╱†
♥	902	♥	╱
0	924		╱
H	926	H	
Z	927	z	
~	928		
◯	935		╱
✱	938		╱*
◪	3041		
S	3042		
O	3045		
T	3046	T	
╱	3047		
▢	3078		
	3328		╱*
⊠	3363		
▣	3712		
⌗	3726		
⟋	3727		
◈	3740		▢
）	3743		
∩	3768	∩	
◐	3772		
✕	3773		
⦂	3774		
▲	3787		╱
◿	5282		╱*
●	3768	French Knot	

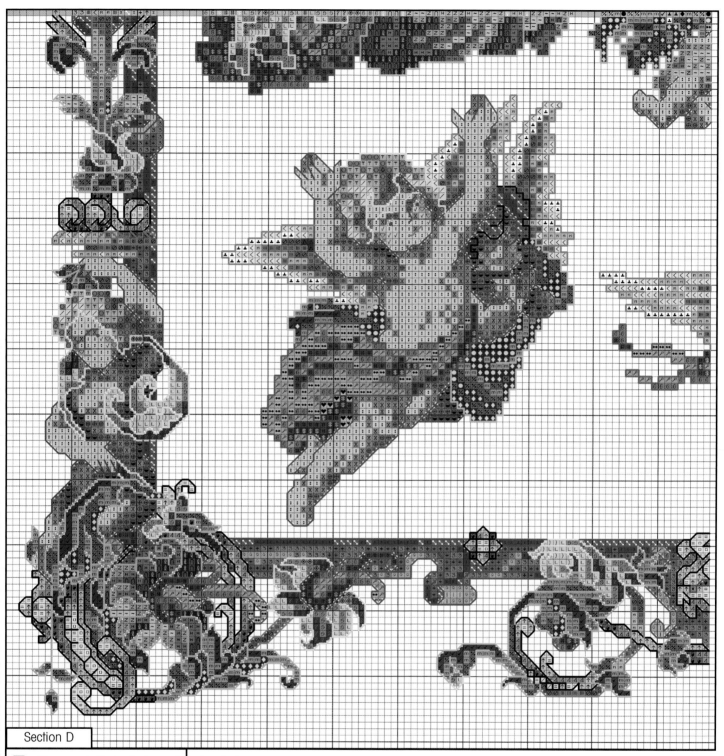

Section D

Blue area indicates last row of previous section of design.

* Use 632 for flesh. Use 938 for all other.

† For lantern strings, work in long stitches.

* Use 3328 for mouths. Use 5282 for all other.

Cherub Ornament (shown on page 33): A portion of the design (refer to photo) was stitched over 2 fabric threads on an 8" square of Zweigart® Cream Cashel Linen® (28 ct). Two strands of floss were used for Cross Stitch and 1 strand for Backstitch. To complete ornament, see Finishing Instructions, page 84.

Cherubs Pillow (shown on page 32): A portion of the design (refer to photo) was stitched over 2 fabric threads on a 16"square of Zweigart® Cream Lugana (25 ct). Three strands of floss were used for Cross Stitch and 1 strand for Backstitch. To complete pillow, see Finishing Instructions, page 84.

chorus of angels

Section E

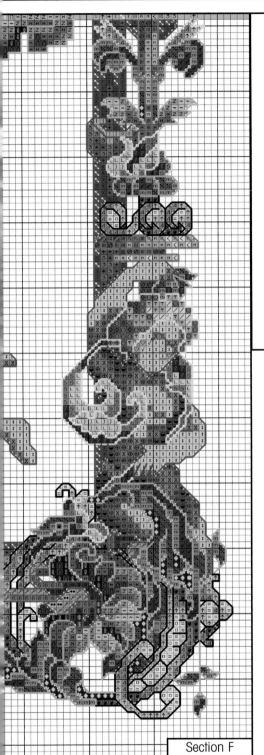

Section F

X	DMC	¼X	B'ST	X	DMC	¼X	B'ST	X	DMC	¼X	B'ST
⊥	blanc	⊥		√	761			⊠	3363		
L	211			↔	778			▣	3712		
$	315	s		⑥	781			#	3726		
6	316			4	783			⌐	3727		
⊕	407			◣	801			◇	3740		⬜
◇	420			<	822			)	3743		
Ⅱ	433		▱	➡	869		▱†	⋂	3768		
✚	435			♥	902		▱	◔	3772		
3	436			◐	924		▱	⊠	3773		
◔	437			H	926			⋮	3774		
◈	520			Z	927			◭	3787		▱
m	523	m		~	928			◿	5282		▱★
✔	524			◯	935		▱	●	3768	French Knot	
	632		▱★	✳	938		▱★	⬜	Blue area indicates last row previous section of design.		
⊘	640			◪	3041						
Ⅲ	642			S	3042			* Use 632 for flesh. Use 938 for all other.			
n	644	n		◯	3045						
↑	725			T	3046	T		† For lantern strings, work in long stitches.			
=	727			▱	3047						
I	738			▢	3078			* Use 3328 for mouths. Use 5282 for all other.			
♡	760				3328		▱★				

Diagram

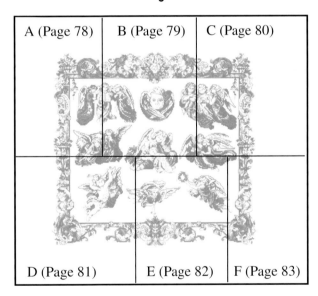

A (Page 78)	B (Page 79)	C (Page 80)
D (Page 81)	E (Page 82)	F (Page 83)

chorus of angels

FINISHING INSTRUCTIONS

Cherub Ornament (shown on page 33, chart on page 79).

For ornament, you will need a 6" dia. circle of fabric for backing, two 4" dia. circles of adhesive mounting board, two 4" dia. circles of batting, 27" length of 1/4" dia. purchased satin cord, 4" tassel, and clear-drying craft glue.

Centering design, trim stitched piece to a 6" dia. circle.

Remove paper from one piece of mounting board and press one batting piece onto mounting board. Repeat with remaining mounting board and batting piece.

Clip 3/8" into edge of stitched piece at 1/2" intervals. Center stitched piece over batting on one mounting board piece; fold edges of stitched piece to back of mounting board and glue in place. For ornament back, repeat with backing fabric and remaining mounting board.

Beginning at bottom center and ending at top center of stitched piece, glue cord to edge of ornament. **Do not cut cord.** For hanger, refer to photo and form 3 loops out of cord; tack loops in place. Continue to glue remaining cord to side of ornament, overlapping ends of cord at bottom center. Referring to photo, glue tassel to back of ornament front. Matching wrong sides, glue ornament front and back together.

Cherubs Pillow (shown on page 32, chart on page 81).

For pillow, you will need an 18" x 12" piece of fabric for backing, two 9" x 12" pieces of fabric for side borders, two 15" lengths of 1/2"w braid, 62" length of 1/4" dia. purchased cording with attached seam allowance, four 1 1/8" dia. ready-to-cover buttons, 4 fabric pieces for buttons, polyester fiberfill, tracing paper, and fabric marking pencil.

For patterns, photocopy Patterns A and B, enlarging them 200%. Trace patterns onto tracing paper; add a 1/2" seam allowance on all sides and cut out patterns. Referring to photo for placement, position Pattern A on wrong side of stitched piece; pin pattern in place. Use fabric marking pencil to draw around pattern; remove pattern and cut out.

For left side border, position Pattern B on wrong side of desired fabric; pin pattern in place. Use fabric marking pencil to draw around pattern; remove pattern and cut out. For right side border, flip Pattern B and repeat with other fabric piece.

Note: When piecing pillow, always match right sides and raw edges. Use a 1/2" seam allowance for all seams.

For pillow front, match long edges and sew each side border to stitched piece. Referring to photo, sew braid to stitched piece covering seam.

If needed, trim seam allowance of cording to 1/2"; pin cording to right side of pillow front making a 3/8" clip in seam allowance of cording at corners. Ends of cording should overlap approximately 4". Turn overlapped ends of cording toward outside edge of pillow front; baste cording to pillow front.

Leaving an opening for turning, sew pillow front and backing fabric together. Trim seam allowances diagonally at corners; turn pillow right side out, carefully pushing corners outward.

For buttons, follow manufacturer's instructions to cover buttons with fabric. Referring to photo for placement, sew buttons to corners of pillow front. Stuff pillow with polyester fiberfill and blind stitch opening closed.

Chorus of Angels Pillow (shown on page 32, chart on pages 79-80).

For pillow, you will need two 19" squares of fabric for pillow front and back, 31" length of 1/2"w braid, 76" length of 2 1/2" long purchased fringe with attached seam allowance, and polyester fiberfill.

Centering design, trim stitched piece to measure 7 1/2" x 7".

Note: Use a 1/2" seam allowance for all seams.

For pillow front, refer to photo and center stitched piece on one fabric piece; pin in place. Attach stitched piece to fabric using a zigzag stitch. Sew braid around stitched piece, covering raw edges.

For fringe, pin straight edge of fringe to right side of pillow front. Ends of fringe should overlap approximately 2". Baste fringe to pillow front.

Matching right sides and raw edges and leaving an opening for turning, sew pillow front and backing fabric together. Trim seam allowances diagonally at corners; turn pillow right side out, carefully pushing corners outward. Stuff pillow with polyester fiberfill and blind stitch opening closed.

Pattern A

Pattern B

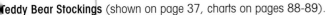

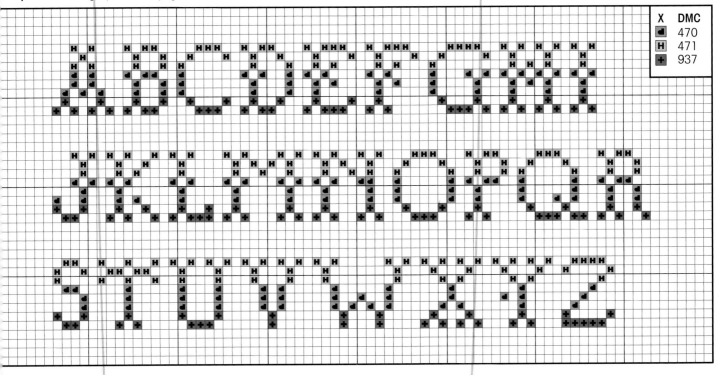

X	DMC
◖	470
H	471
✚	937

FINISHING INSTRUCTIONS

Angel and Old Testament Ornaments (shown on pages 26-27, charts on page 73).

For each ornament, you will need an 8" square of fabric for backing, polyester fiberfill, 14" length of twisted cord for edges, and 8" length of twisted cord for hanger. For Design #1, you will also need two 1¼" tassels. For Design #2, you will also need an 8" length of twisted cord for bow. For Designs #3 and #4, you will also need a 1¼" tassel.

Matching right sides and raw edges, pin stitched piece and backing fabric together. Referring to photo, trim backing fabric and stitched piece **1" larger** than design on all sides. Leaving an opening for turning, use a ½" seam allowance to sew fabric pieces together. Clip seam allowances at corners and curves. Turn ornament right side out, carefully pushing corners and curves outward. Stuff ornament with polyester fiberfill; blind stitch opening closed. Blind stitch cord around edges of ornament.

For hanger, fold cord in half and tie an overhand knot ½" from ends. Referring to photo for placement, sew hanger to top of ornament and tassels or bow to bottom of ornament.

"Hark! The Herald Angels Sing" Pillow (shown on page 26, chart on page 74).

For pillow, you will need a 9¾" dia. piece of fabric for backing, 2½" x 55" fabric strip for ruffle (pieced as necessary), 2" x 29" bias fabric strip for cording, 29" length of ¼" dia. purchased cord, 3" x 9" fabric strip for hanger, 3" x 10" fabric strip for bow, two ⅞" dia. ready-to-cover buttons, 2 fabric pieces for buttons, and polyester fiberfill.

Centering design, trim stitched piece to measure 9¾" dia. circle.

For cording, center cord on wrong side of bias strip; matching long edges, fold strip over cord. Use a zipper foot to baste along length of strip close

to cord; trim seam allowance to ½". Clip ⅜" into seam allowance of cording at ½" intervals. Matching raw edges, pin cording to right side of stitched piece. Ends of cording should overlap approximately 2"; pin overlapping end out of the way. Starting 2" from beginning end of cording and ending 4" from overlapping end, baste cording to stitched piece. On overlapping end of cording, remove 2½" of basting; fold end of fabric back and trim cord so that it meets beginning end of cord. Fold end of fabric ½" to wrong side; wrap fabric over beginning end of cording. Finish basting cording to stitched piece.

For ruffle, press short edges of fabric strip ½" to wrong side. Matching wrong sides and long edges, fold strip in half; press. Machine baste ½" from raw edges; gather fabric strip to fit stitched piece. Matching raw edges, pin ruffle to right side of stitched piece, overlapping short ends ¼". Use a ½" seam allowance to sew ruffle to stitched piece.

Matching right sides and leaving an opening for turning, use a ½" seam allowance to sew stitched piece and backing fabric together. Clip seam allowances; turn pillow right side out. Stuff pillow with polyester fiberfill and blind stitch opening closed.

For buttons, follow manufacturer's instructions to cover buttons with matching fabric. Referring to photo for placement, sew buttons to front and back of pillow.

For hanger, match right sides and raw edges of fabric strip. Using ½" seam allowance, sew long edges together; turn right side out and press. Repeat for bow fabric strip. Fold hanger in half and referring to photo, sew ends to top of pillow. Tie remaining fabric strip into a bow and referring to photo, blind stitch to top of hanger.

BEARING GIFTS

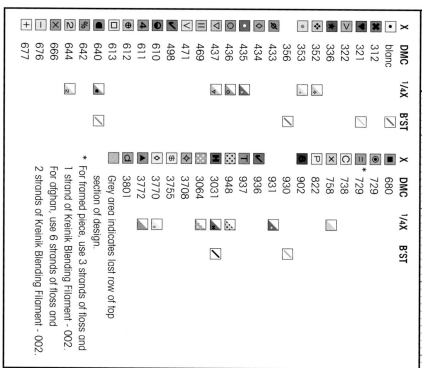

Color key DMC numbers (top section): 677, 676, 666, 644, 642, 640, 613, 612, 611, 610, 498, 471, 469, 437, 436, 435, 434, 433, 356, 353, 352, 336, 322, 321, 312, blanc

Columns: DMC, 1/4X, B'ST

Color key DMC numbers (bottom section): 3801, 3772, 3770, 3755, 3708, 3064, 3031, 948, 937, 936, 931, 930, 902, 822, 758, 738, 729, 680

Columns: DMC, 1/4X, B'ST

Grey area indicates last row of top section of design.

* For framed piece, use 3 strands of floss and
1 strand of Kreinik Blending Filament - 002.
For afghan, use 6 strands of floss and
2 strands of Kreinik Blending Filament - 002.

Bearing Gifts (shown on page 35): The design was stitched over 2 fabric threads on a 15" x 16" piece of Zweigart® Raw Belfast Linen (32 ct). Two strands of floss were used for Cross Stitch and 1 strand for Backstitch, unless otherwise noted in the color key. It was custom framed.

Bearing Gifts Afghan (shown on page 36): The design was stitched over 2 fabric threads on a 45" x 58" piece of Ivory All-Cotton Anne Cloth (18 ct).

For afghan, cut selvages from fabric; measure 5¹⁄₂" from raw edge of fabric and pull out 1 fabric thread. Fringe fabric up to missing fabric thread. Repeat for each side. Tie an overhand knot at each corner with 4 horizontal and 4 vertical fabric threads. Working from corners, use 8 fabric threads for each knot until all threads are knotted.

Refer to Diagram for placement of design on fabric; use 6 strands of floss for Cross Stitch and 2 strands for Backstitch, unless otherwise noted in the color key.

Design by Carol Emmer.

DIAGRAM

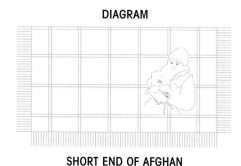

SHORT END OF AFGHAN

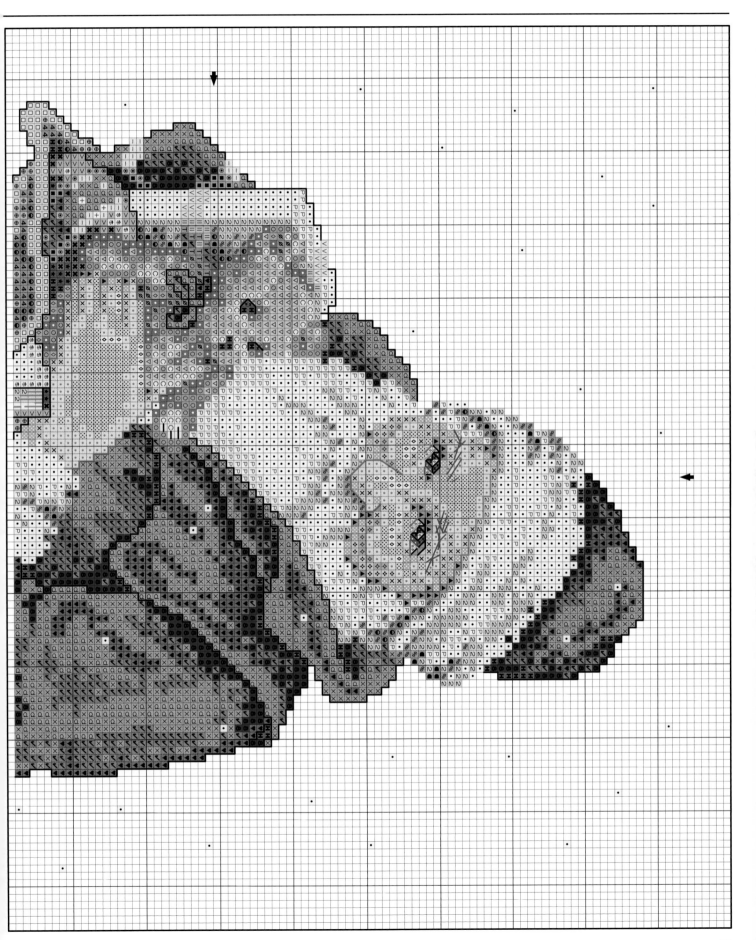

BEARING GIFTS

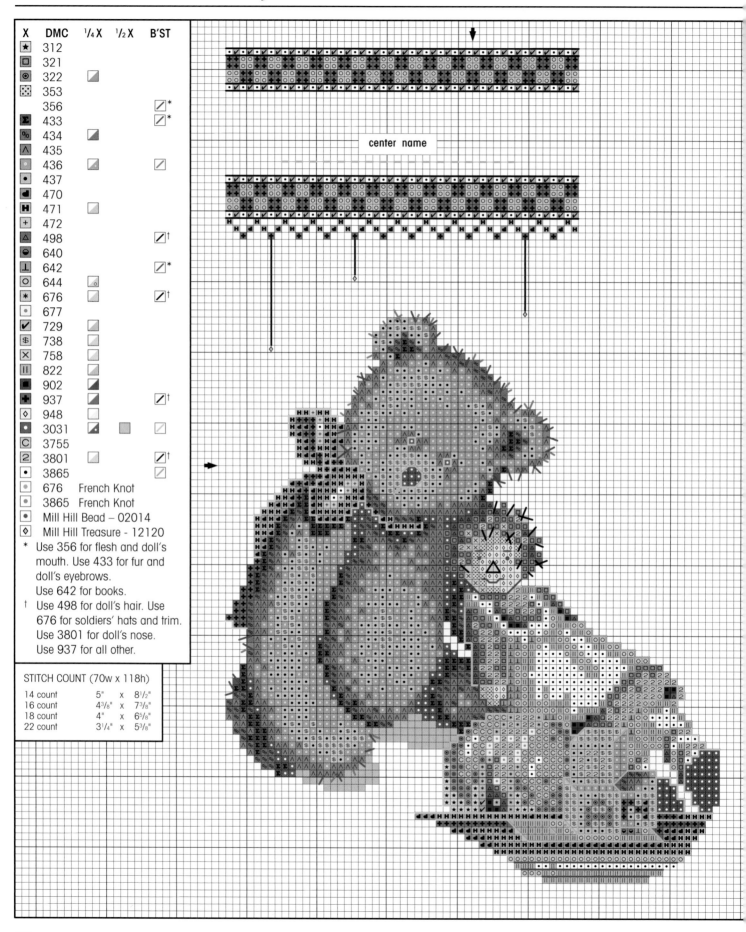

X	DMC	1/4 X	1/2 X	B'ST
★	312			
□	321			
⊙	322	◪		
⋰	353			
	356			◹ *
Σ	433			◹ *
%	434	◪		
∧	435			
◨	436	◪		◹
•	437			
◢	470			
H	471	◪		
+	472			
△	498			◹ †
◉	640			
⊥	642			◹ *
○	644	◪		
✳	676			◹ †
·	677			
✔	729	◪		
$	738	◪		
✕	758	◪		
‖	822	◪		
■	902	◪		
✚	937	◪		◹ †
◇	948	◪		
▣	3031	◪	▨	◹
C	3755			
2	3801	◪		◹ †
•	3865			◹

⊙	676	French Knot
◉	3865	French Knot
•	Mill Hill Bead – 02014	
◇	Mill Hill Treasure – 12120	

* Use 356 for flesh and doll's mouth. Use 433 for fur and doll's eyebrows. Use 642 for books.

† Use 498 for doll's hair. Use 676 for soldiers' hats and trim. Use 3801 for doll's nose. Use 937 for all other.

STITCH COUNT (70w x 118h)

14 count	5"	x	8½"
16 count	4⅜"	x	7⅜"
18 count	4"	x	6⅝"
22 count	3¼"	x	5⅜"

center name

center name

STITCH COUNT (69w x 118h)

14 count	5"	x 8½"
16 count	4⅜"	x 7⅜"
18 count	3⅞"	x 6⅝"
22 count	3¼"	x 5⅜"

Teddy Bear Stockings (shown on page 37): Each design was stitched over 2 fabric threads on a 14" x 18" piece of Zweigart® Cream Lugana (25 ct). Two strands of floss were used for Cross Stitch and 1 strand for Half Cross Stitch, Backstitch, and French Knots. Attach beads using 1 strand of DMC 310 floss. See Attaching Beads, page 96. Attach treasures using 1 strand of DMC 436 floss. Personalize stocking using alphabet provided on page 85.

For each stocking, you will need a 14" x 18" piece of fabric for backing, two 14" x 18" pieces of fabric for lining, 25" length of ¼" dia. purchased cording with attached seam allowance, 2" x 6" piece of fabric for hanger, tracing paper, pencil, and fabric marking pencil.

Trace Stocking Pattern, page 85, onto tracing paper; add ½" seam allowance on all sides and cut out pattern. Referring to photo, position pattern on wrong side of stitched piece; pin pattern in place. Use fabric marking pencil to draw around pattern; remove pattern and cut out on drawn line. Use pattern and cut **one** from backing fabric and **two** from lining fabric.

If needed, trim seam allowance of cording to ½". Matching raw edges, baste cording to right side of stocking front.

Matching right sides and leaving top edge open, use a ½" seam allowance to sew stitched piece and backing fabric together. Clip seam allowance at curves and turn stocking right side out. Press top edge of stocking ½" to wrong side.

Matching right sides and leaving top edge open, use a ⅝" seam allowance to sew lining pieces together; trim seam allowance close to stitching. **Do not turn lining right side out.** Press top edge of lining ½" to wrong side.

For hanger, press each long edge of fabric strip ½" to center. Matching long edges, fold strip in half and sew close to folded edges. Matching short edges, fold hanger in half and whipstitch to inside of stocking at left seam.

With wrong sides facing, place lining inside stocking; blind stitch lining to stocking.

Designs by Carol Emmer.

MADONNA AND CHILD

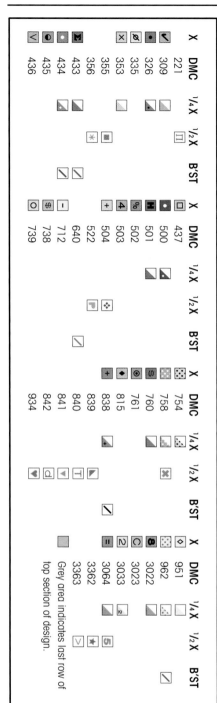

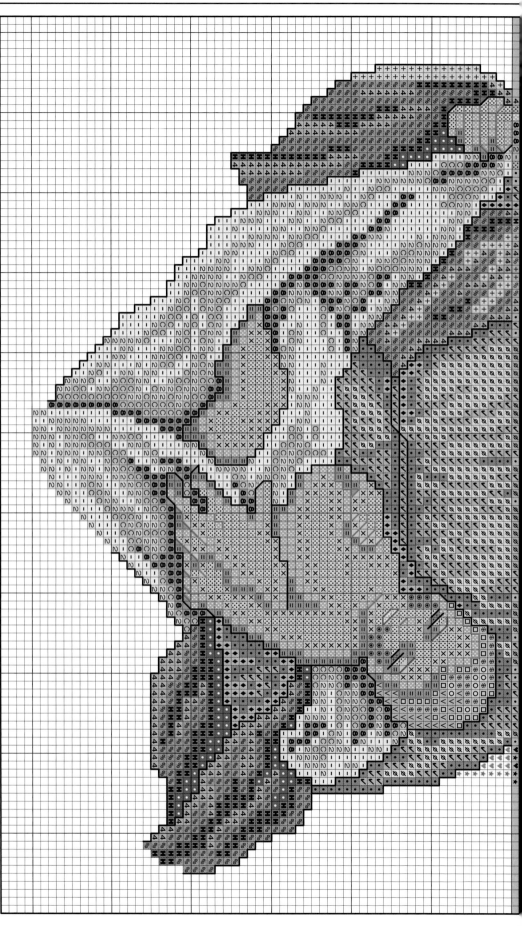

Madonna and Child in Frame (shown on page 39): The design was stitched over 2 fabric threads on a 16" x 20" piece of Zweigart® Cream Lugana (25 ct). Three strands of floss were used for Cross Stitch and 1 strand for Half Cross Stitch and Backstitch. It was custom framed.

Needlework adaptation by Carol Emmer.

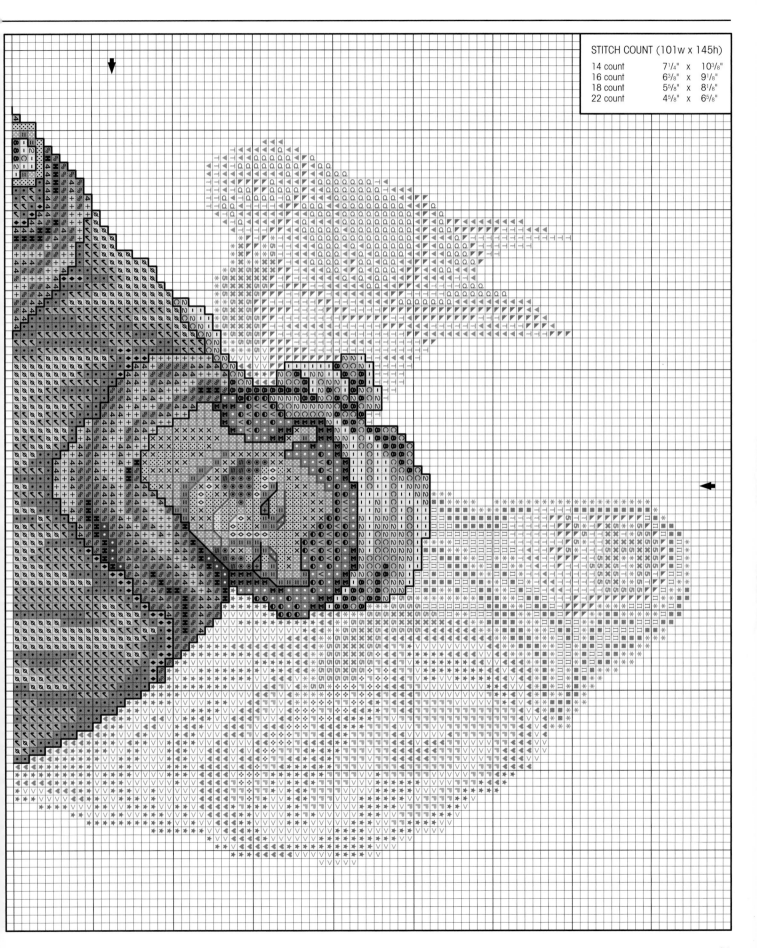

STITCH COUNT (101w x 145h)

14 count	7¼"	x	10³⁄₈"
16 count	6³⁄₈"	x	9¹⁄₈"
18 count	5⁵⁄₈"	x	8¹⁄₈"
22 count	4⁵⁄₈"	x	6⁵⁄₈"

CHRISTMAS BOTANICALS

X	DMC	¼X	B'ST		X	DMC	¼X	B'ST		X	DMC	¼X	B'ST
∅	351				■	816		✓		=	955		
☐	353				+	817		+		✗	3341		
2	469		✓			839		✓			3818		✓
⊓	471				♡	841				☆	3820		
•	472				◐	910				•	841		French Knot
P	745				V	913		✓					

STITCH COUNT (85w x 100h)

14 count	6⅛"	x	7¼"
16 count	5⅜"	x	6¼"
18 count	4¾"	x	5⅝"
22 count	3⅞"	x	4⅝"

X	DMC	¼X	X	DMC	¼X	B'ST	X	DMC	¼X	B'ST
•	blanc	•	V	704			◉	986		
✚	304		=	772			✕	3341		
■	606			816		✓	2	3346		✓
○	642		▣	839		✓	•	839		French Knot
◓	702		▽	841						

Poinsettia and Holly in Frames (shown on pages 40-41): Each design was stitched over 2 fabric threads on a 14" x 15" piece of Zweigart® Antique White Cashel Linen® (28 ct). Two strands of floss were used for Cross Stitch and 1 strand for Backstitch and French Knots. They were custom framed.

Designs by Jorja Hernandez.

93

Children in the Snow

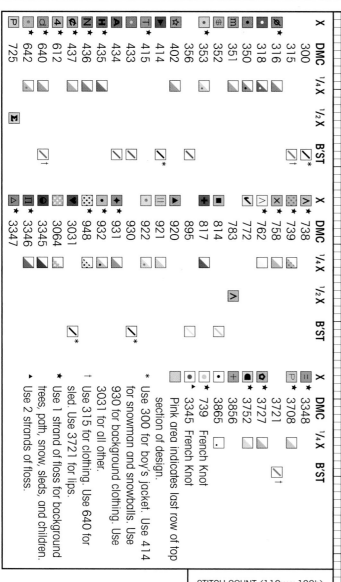

X	DMC	1/4X	1/2X	B'ST
	300			✓*
	315			✓†
★	316	✓		
	318	✓		
	350	✓		
	351	✓		
	352			
★	353	✓		
	356			✓
	402	✓		
	414			✓*
★	415			
	433			✓
	434			✓
★	435	✓		
★	436	✓		
★	437	✓		
★	612			
★	640	✓		✓†
★	642	✓		
	725		✓	

X	DMC	1/4X	1/2X	B'ST
★	738			
★	739	✓		
★	758	✓		
★	762	✓		
	772			
	783		✓	
	814			✓
	817	✓		
	895			✓
	920			
	921	✓		
	922	✓		
	930			✓*
★	931	✓		
★	932	✓		
★	948	✓		
	3031			✓*
	3064	✓		
	3345	✓		
★	3346	✓		
★	3347			

X	DMC	1/4X	B'ST
★	3348		
★	3708	✓	
	3721		✓†
★	3727	✓	
★	3752	✓	
	3856		
	3865	✓	
★	739 French Knot		
▲	3345 French Knot		
	Pink area indicates last row of top section of design.		

* Use 300 for boy's jacket. Use 414 for snowman and snowballs. Use 930 for background clothing. Use 3031 for all other.

† Use 315 for clothing. Use 640 for sled. Use 3721 for lips.

★ Use 1 strand of floss for background trees, path, snow, sleds, and children.

▲ Use 2 strands of floss.

STITCH COUNT (110w x 133h)			
14 count	7⅞"	x	9½"
16 count	6⅞"	x	8⅜"
18 count	6⅛"	x	7½"
22 count	5"	x	6⅛"

Children in the Snow in Frame (shown on page 43): The design was stitched over 2 fabric threads on a 16" x 18" piece of Zweigart® Platinum Cashel Linen® (28 ct). Two strands of floss were used for Cross Stitch and 1 strand for Half Cross Stitch, Backstitch, and French Knots, unless otherwise noted in the color key. It was custom framed.

Design by Carol Emmer.

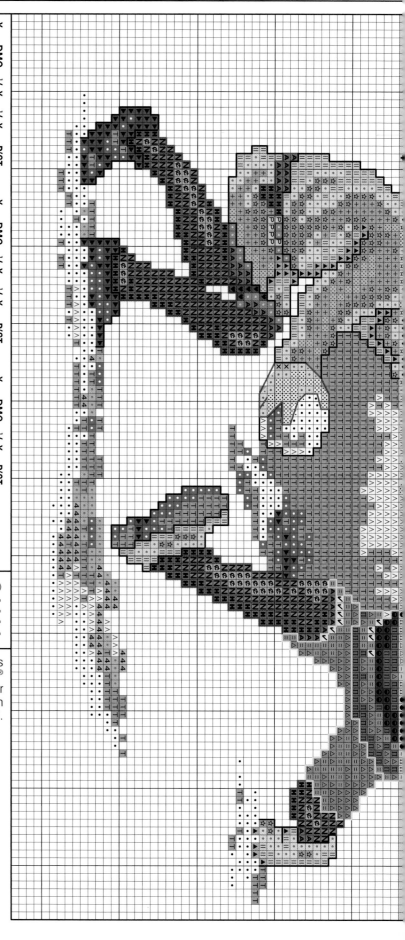

GENERAL INSTRUCTIONS

WORKING WITH CHARTS

How to Read Charts: Each of the designs is shown in chart form. Each colored square on the chart represents one Cross Stitch or one Half Cross Stitch. Each colored triangle on the chart represents one One-Quarter Stitch or one Three-Quarter Stitch. In some charts, reduced symbols are used to indicate One-Quarter Stitches (**Fig. 1**). **Fig. 2** and **Fig. 3** indicate Cross Stitch under Backstitch.

Fig. 1   **Fig. 2**   **Fig. 3**

Black or colored dots on the chart represent Cross Stitch, French Knots, or bead placement. The black or colored straight lines on the chart indicate Backstitch. The symbol is omitted or reduced when a French Knot, Backstitch, or bead covers a square.

Each chart is accompanied by a color key. This key indicates the color of floss to use for each stitch on the chart. The headings on the color key are for Cross Stitch (**X**), DMC color number (**DMC**), One-Quarter Stitch (**¼X**), Three-Quarter Stitch (**¾X**), Half Cross Stitch (**½X**), and Backstitch (**B'ST**). Color key columns should be read vertically and horizontally to determine type of stitch and floss color. Some designs may include stitches worked with metallic thread, such as blending filament, braid, or cord. The metallic thread may be blended with floss or used alone. If any metallic thread is used in a design, the color key will contain the necessary information.

STITCHING TIP

Attaching Beads: Refer to chart for bead placement and sew bead in place using a fine needle that will pass through bead. Bring needle up at 1, run needle through bead and then down at 2. Secure floss on back or move to next bead as shown in **Fig. 4**.

Fig. 4

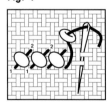

STITCH DIAGRAMS

Note: Bring threaded needle up at 1 and all odd numbers and down at 2 and all even numbers.

Counted Cross Stitch (X): Work one Cross Stitch to correspond to each colored square on the chart. For horizontal rows, work stitches in two journeys (**Fig. 5**). For vertical rows, complete each stitch as shown (**Fig. 6**). When working over two fabric threads, work Cross Stitch as shown in **Fig. 7**. When the chart shows a Backstitch crossing a colored square (**Fig. 8**), a Cross Stitch should be worked first; then the Backstitch (**Fig. 13** or **14**) should be worked on top of the Cross Stitch.

Fig. 5   **Fig. 6**

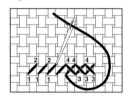

Fig. 7   **Fig. 8**

Quarter Stitch (¼X and ¾X): Quarter Stitches are denoted by triangular shapes of color on the chart and on the color key. For a One-Quarter Stitch, come up at 1 (**Fig. 9**), then split fabric thread to go down at 2. When stitches 1-4 are worked in the same color, the resulting stitch is called a Three-Quarter Stitch (**¾X**). **Fig. 10** shows the technique for Quarter Stitches when working over two fabric threads.

Fig. 9   **Fig. 10**

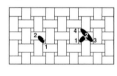 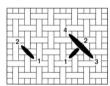

Half Cross Stitch (½X): This stitch is one journey of the Cross Stitch and is worked from lower left to upper right as shown in **Fig. 11**. When working over two fabric threads, work Half Cross Stitch as shown in **Fig. 12**.

Fig. 11   **Fig. 12**

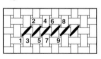

Backstitch (B'ST): For outline detail, Backstitch (shown on chart and on color key by black or colored straight lines) should be worked after the design has been completed (**Fig. 13**). When working over two fabric threads, work Backstitch as shown in **Fig. 14**.

Fig. 13   **Fig. 14**

 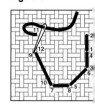

French Knot: Bring needle up at 1. Wrap floss once around needle and insert needle [at] 2, holding end of floss with non-stitching finger (**Fig. 15**). Tighten knot, then pull needle through fabric, holding floss until it must be released. For larger knot, use more strands of floss; wrap only once.

Fig. 15

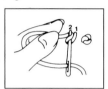

Lazy Daisy Stitch: Bring needle up at 1 [and] make a loop. Go down at 1 and come up [at] 2, keeping floss below point of needle (**Fig. 16**). Pull needle through and go down [at] 2 to anchor loop, completing stitch. (**Note:** [For] support stitches, it may be helpful to [go] down in edge of next fabric thread w[hen] anchoring loop.)

Fig. 16

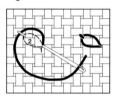

Satin Stitch: This stitch is a series of straight stitches worked side by side (**Fig. 17**). [The] number of threads worked over and [the] direction of stitches will vary according [to] the chart.

Fig. 17

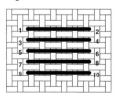

Photo models were stitched using DMC floss, courtesy of The DMC Corporation.

Instructions tested and photo items made [by] Kandi Ashford, Muriel Hicks, Stephanie Gail Sh[...], Anne Simpson, Lavonne Sims, Helen Stanton, [...] Trish Vines.